HAPGOOD

HAPGOOD

TOM STOPPARD

faber and faber
LONDON · BOSTON

First published in 1988
by Faber and Faber Limited
3 Queen Square London WC1N 3AU

Typeset by Wilmaset, Birkenhead, Wirral
Printed in Great Britain by
Richard Clay Ltd Bungay Suffolk
All rights reserved

British Library Cataloguing in Publication Data

Stoppard, Tom
Hapgood.
I. Title
822'.914   PR6069.T6

ISBN 0–571–15159–0
ISBN 0–571–15160–4 Pbk

For Oliver with love and thanks

We choose to examine a phenomenon which is impossible, *absolutely* impossible, to explain in any classical way, and which has in it the heart of quantum mechanics. In reality it contains the *only* mystery . . . Any other situation in quantum mechanics, it turns out, can always be explained by saying, 'You remember the case of the experiment with the two holes? It's the same thing.'

Richard P. Feynman
'Lectures on Physics'/'The Character of Physical Law'

CHARACTERS

HAPGOOD	aged thirty-eight
BLAIR	probably twenty years older, but in good shape.
KERNER	forty-ish
RIDLEY	mid-thirties
WATES	either side of forty-five
MAGGS	twenties
MERRYWEATHER	twenty-two
JOE	eleven
RUSSIAN	any age, thirty to fifty

ACT ONE

ACT TWO

Hapgood was presented by Michael Codron at the Aldwych Theatre, London, on 8 March 1988. The cast was as follows:

HAPGOOD	Felicity Kendal
BLAIR	Nigel Hawthorne
KERNER	Roger Rees
RIDLEY	Iain Glen
WATES	Al Matthews
MERRYWEATHER	Adam Norton
MAGGS	Roger Gartland
JOE	Christopher Price *or* Andrew Read
RUSSIAN	Patrick Gordon

Directed by Peter Wood
Designed by Carl Toms
Lighting by David Hersey

ACT ONE

SCENE I

We are looking at part of the men's changing room of an old-fashioned municipal swimming-baths. It is ten o'clock in the morning. The cubicles are numbered, and they have doors which conceal occupancy although they don't meet the ground. There is a washbasin or two, a place to shave facing front. Four of the cubicles have to 'work'.

There are four ways of coming and going: 'Lobby', 'Pool', 'Showers', and, for the sake of argument, 'Upstage'.

The lobby doors have MEN *in reverse on the glass. Signs saying* POOL, SHOWERS, GENTS *and* EXIT *may be used.*

One of the showers is evidently in use – we can hear it. When we encounter this scene, WATES *is shaving. He is a black man, an American, who is normally impressively tailored and suave but at present is dressed in cast-offs and looks as if he spent last night on a park bench. His tackle is basic – shaving brush, shaving stick, old-fashioned safety razor.*

Before anything else happens we have a short radio play. What we can hear is two people (a man and a woman, HAPGOOD) *talking to each other on shortwave radio. The voices accordingly have a slight distort.*

RADIO: OK, we have a blue Peugeot . . . stopping.

    Single male.

    It's not Georgi.

    Anybody know him? Carrying a towel, no briefcase, repeat negative on briefcase.

    Are you getting this, Mother? – we have the Peugeot but it's not Georgi.

    He's crossing the road. Fancy tracksuit, running shoes. No sign of the follower.

    Are you getting this? – target is approaching, negative on Georgi, negative on briefcase, negative on follower, give me a colour.

HAPGOOD: (*On* RADIO) Green. You should be seeing Kerner.

I

RADIO: Negative. They changed the plot. Confirm green.

HAPGOOD: (*On* RADIO) Green. Tell me when Kerner shows.

WATES: (*Live*) *If* he shows.

HAPGOOD: (*On* RADIO) Tell me when Kerner shows, he'll be walking.

WATES: (*Live; no emotion*) Kerner is thirty thousand feet up on Aeroflot, I feel sick.

RADIO: Who the heck is that?

HAPGOOD: (*On* RADIO) Wates – just shave.

WATES: (*Live*) Yes, ma'am.

RADIO: Target inside. Negative on Kerner. Target in lobby. Ridley has seen him. Still negative on Kerner. Do I hear yellow? Mother, give me a colour, we're still –

OK, we have a walker.

OK, we have Kerner . . . three hundred yards . . . affirmative on briefcase.

Target's got his key.

HAPGOOD: (*On* RADIO) Say when.

RADIO: Four – three – two –

(*The lobby door opens.*)

You're looking at him.

(*A* MAN *enters from the lobby. He wears a colourful tracksuit and running shoes. He carries a towel rolled up into a sausage, we assume the swimming trunks and cap are inside. He carries a key on a loop of string which might make it convenient to wear as a pendant. He is otherwise empty-handed. We call this man* RUSSIAN ONE, *because he is Russian and because there are going to be two of them.*

RUSSIAN ONE *enters Cubicle One. [This numbering has nothing to do with the actual numbers on the cubicles, it is only for our convenience.]* RUSSIAN ONE *enters his cubicle and closes the door behind him.*

RIDLEY *enters from the lobby. He is carrying a briefcase [but the briefcase may be inside a sports holdall].* RIDLEY *now goes on a perambulation. The essence of the situation is that* RIDLEY *moves around and through, in view and out of view, demonstrating that the place as a whole is variously circumnavigable in a way which will later recall, if not replicate, the problem of the bridges of Königsberg [and which will give* RUSSIAN ONE *time to undress]. It is possible that on his entrance* RIDLEY *will dump his briefcase into a laundry basket overflowing with used towels, and then reclaim it when he has finished coming and going.*

Back to the plot. RUSSIAN ONE, *dressed to swim, leaves his cubicle, locks it, swings his towel up over the lintel and leaves it hanging there, and goes off to the pool. When he has gone,* RIDLEY *posts his briefcase under the door of Cubicle One, and pulls the towel off the door. [As a matter of interest, the* RIDLEY *who posts the briefcase is not the same* RIDLEY *who entered with it.]* RIDLEY *enters Cubicle Two and closes the door behind him. The towel appears, flung over the lintel, hanging down.*

WATES *continues to shave. The shower continues to run.*

KERNER *enters from the lobby. He carries a briefcase. He has a towel and a key. He looks around and posts his briefcase under the door with the towel showing [Cubicle Two].*

KERNER *pulls the towel off the door and tosses it over the door into the cubicle.* KERNER *enters another cubicle [Cubicle Three] and closes the door behind him. A moment later his towel appears over the lintel.*

RIDLEY *leaves Cubicle Two, bringing Kerner's briefcase with him, and also the towel. He chucks the towel over the door of Cubicle One. With the briefcase he disappears in the direction of the showers. The shower cubicle may be in full view.*

RUSSIAN ONE *leaves the pool, wet of course, and re-enters his cubicle.*

RIDLEY *comes back into view, from the showers, without the briefcase. He goes to the pool.*

RUSSIAN TWO *enters from the lobby. He is the twin of* RUSSIAN ONE, *and dressed like* RUSSIAN ONE. *He carries a similar rolled-up towel. However, he also carries a briefcase. He glances round briefly, and notes the towel on Kerner's door. He posts his briefcase under Kerner's door. He enters a cubicle, Cubicle Four.*

3

MERRYWEATHER, *a boyish twenty-two-year-old in sports jacket and flannels, enters from the lobby. His manner is not as well calculated as* RIDLEY's *had been. He is at first relieved and then immediately disconcerted by the absence of Russians.*
RUSSIAN ONE, *now dressed, leaves his cubicle, carrying his rolled-up towel but leaving the briefcase [which Ridley posted] behind.* RUSSIAN ONE *leaves to the lobby.*
MERRYWEATHER, *whose idea of making himself inconspicuous has been, perhaps, to examine himself in* WATES's *mirror, follows* RUSSIAN ONE *out to the lobby.*
KERNER, *dressed, leaves Cubicle Three, with the briefcase which had been posted there, and leaves to the lobby.*
RUSSIAN TWO *reappears, from Cubicle Four, and enters Cubicle One to collect the briefcase which had been left in there. As he leaves the cubicle,* RIDLEY *re-enters from the pool.*
RUSSIAN TWO *leaves to the lobby.* RIDLEY *follows him out.*
WATES *has finished shaving. He is packing up his shaving tackle.*
The shower stops running. There is a pause, and then the occupant of the shower, HAPGOOD, *approaches, somewhat encumbered by a briefcase [Kerner's original], a leather rectangular clutch handbag with a shoulder strap, and an umbrella which she is at the moment taking down and shaking out. From her appearance, the umbrella has been an entire success. She comes down into the light and leans the umbrella carefully against the cubicles, and stands pensively for a moment. She is apparently too preoccupied to acknowledge* WATES, *who is himself preoccupied with something which makes him shake with silent laughter. He is putting a heavy steel wrist-watch on his right wrist. [NOTE: In the first production, all the foregoing action was done to music and lightly choreographed.])*

WATES: Young guy in a sports coat, college haircut, nasty wart on the back of his right hand, no, left, it was in the mirror.

HAPGOOD: Merryweather.

WATES: Merryweather, right. Followed the man in, followed the wrong man out, meanwhile Merryweather's man turns around and leaves with the goods. Sort of dummy.

HAPGOOD: Yes, he is rather.

(*The lobby doors open.* RIDLEY *enters in a somewhat excited, even delighted, state.*)

RIDLEY: (*Greeting her*) Mother.

HAPGOOD: This is Ridley.

RIDLEY: You didn't tell me it was twins.

HAPGOOD: This is Wates.

(HAPGOOD *puts the briefcase on the ground, then lays it flat. She undoes the catches and raises the lid. During this* WATES *and* RIDLEY *shake hands.*)

WATES: Ben Wates.

RIDLEY: (*Friendly*) Ridley.

(HAPGOOD *has stood up, taking from the case a flat white cardboard box, a few inches square, the sort of thing that might contain a computer disc, which is what in fact it does contain. However, she is not in the slightest interested in the box. She stands staring down at the open briefcase.*

RIDLEY *has just said, 'Ridley'. The lobby doors open to admit* MERRYWEATHER – *but only momentarily because all* MERRYWEATHER *sees is a young woman with her face turned away from him and he makes the modest assumption that he has walked through the wrong door.*)

MERRYWEATHER: Oh, God, I'm terribly –

(*He's gone again.* HAPGOOD *hasn't moved.*)

HAPGOOD: Sugar! . . . Wates.

(*Now* WATES *looks at her and at the briefcase.*)

WATES: Oh, Lord.

(MERRYWEATHER *puts his head in the door, somewhat tentatively.* HAPGOOD *tosses the disc-box back into the briefcase.*)

HAPGOOD: Where's yours, Ridley?

RIDLEY: In the Peugeot.

MERRYWEATHER: (*Advancing*) Oh hello, Mother – I didn't rea–

HAPGOOD: Where did he go, Merryweather?

MERRYWEATHER: Actually, I lost him – a taxi came round the

corner –

HAPGOOD: He's in the taxi?

(MERRYWEATHER *nods*.)

RIDLEY: (*To* HAPGOOD) Chamberlain's cab, I love it. Listen, how the hell –

HAPGOOD: (*Politely*) Be quiet, Ridley.

(*She is opening her handbag and taking out a small radio transmitter/receiver.*

These gadgets are going to get quite a lot of use and evidently the state of the art has arrived at a radio which is no larger and somewhat slimmer than twenty cigarettes. The radio speaks quietly.

So HAPGOOD *is taking her radio out of her handbag.*)

(*To* MERRYWEATHER) Have a look round the pool.

MERRYWEATHER: Right. What for exactly?

HAPGOOD: Anything there is, I'll want to see it. (*To* RADIO) Cotton.

RADIO: Mother.

(WATES *and* MERRYWEATHER *dovetail with* HAPGOOD *and her radio.*)

WATES: (*Shaking hands*) Ben Wates.

MERRYWEATHER: How do you do, sir? Merryweather.

(MERRYWEATHER *goes out to the pool.* RIDLEY *is probably contemplating the briefcase.*

WATES *moves quietly up towards the cubicles and calmly investigates them, one after another without fuss.*

During this:)

HAPGOOD: (*To* RADIO) Where is he?

RADIO: In the Peugeot.

HAPGOOD: (*Patiently*) Thank you, Cotton, and where is the Peugeot?

RADIO: Camden High Street.

HAPGOOD: Pick him up and I want everything, I want him in a plastic bag.

RADIO: Yes, ma'am.

HAPGOOD: Contents of briefcase. I'm here to be told.

RADIO: You know it's twins?

6

HAPGOOD: Yes, I know it's twins.

(*To* RIDLEY) You take Kerner – go through him, do it properly.

(*To* RADIO) Who's got the taxi?

RIDLEY: Kerner's clean.

RADIO: Mother.

RIDLEY: I did the switch.

HAPGOOD: (*To* RIDLEY, *more sharply*) Move.

(RIDLEY *exits to the lobby.*)

HAPGOOD: (*To* RADIO) Where is he?

RADIO: It isn't he, it's *them.*

HAPGOOD: Thank you, I heard. Where's yours?

RADIO: Chalk Farm, turning west on Adelaide.

HAPGOOD: Bring him in.

RADIO: It's a bit public.

HAPGOOD: Can't be helped, do it.

RADIO: Yes, Mother.

HAPGOOD: I'm here to be told. (*She turns the gadget off, hesitates, and turns it on again. To* RADIO) Paul . . .
(*Her tone for Paul is different – she is not giving orders. No answer.*) Paul . . .
(*Still no answer. She turns the* RADIO *off.*
WATES *is coming back to her.*)
Is the briefcase right?

WATES: It's right. I guess we took our eye off the ball.
(HAPGOOD *picks up the disc-box from the open briefcase. She opens the little box – it is sealed and to open it you have to tear a strip away, the way a Jiffy-bag works; it's a once-only box. She does this, and takes out the disc, and then replaces it in the box, and replaces the box in the briefcase which she then closes. During this:*)

HAPGOOD: What about the bleep?

WATES: It's dead.

HAPGOOD: I'll need the time.

WATES: You'll get it. Why didn't he take the disc?

HAPGOOD: Who?

WATES: Whoever.

(HAPGOOD *goes to collect her umbrella.*)

HAPGOOD: (*To* RADIO) I'm leaving.

RADIO: Car out front.

HAPGOOD: (*To* RADIO) Thank you. (*She puts the radio back into her bag.*)

Wates . . .

WATES: Yes, ma'am.

HAPGOOD: Thank you for your co-operation.

WATES: You bet.

(*He holds the briefcase out for her and she takes it.*)

HAPGOOD: Well, we'll talk. You're invited.

WATES: Appreciate it.

(HAPGOOD *starts off to the lobby door.* MERRYWEATHER *comes back in from the pool.*)

MERRYWEATHER: Nothing, Mother – the whole place is clean.

HAPGOOD: (*Continuing out*) Drain the pool.

(*The doors swing behind her.*)

MERRYWEATHER: (*Thoughtfully, not entirely happy*) Drain the pool.

(*He goes back to the pool.* WATES *is alone. He is evidently a man with a burden. He is getting ready to leave, perhaps he has a coat to put on. From the pocket he takes a similar radio and walks towards the doors, raising the radio to his mouth; at which point everything changes for him. He stops to listen, his head turned back towards the upstage, by which time, gracefully and without making a big thing of it, he has tossed his radio from right hand to left, and produced from somewhere about his person a short-barrelled revolver. He stands listening, holding the gun down by his side. He has to be patient but after a while a figure comes out of the dark upstage between the cubicles. This turns out to be a man wearing a hat and a good tweed overcoat, his hands in the pockets, a slightly surprising colourful silk scarf tucked inside the coat. He walks down in his own time, a careful stroll.* WATES *does not move until the downstage light falls across* BLAIR's *face.* BLAIR *comes to a halt.* WATES *puts his gun away, gets the radio back into his right hand and resumes.*)

8

WATES: (*To* RADIO) Wates – I need the sweeps.
    (*He nods at* BLAIR.)
    Paul.
BLAIR: (*Greets him back*) Ben.
RADIO: Sweeps coming up.
WATES: (*To* RADIO) Thank you.
    (*He puts the radio in his pocket and, in leaving, speaks to*
    BLAIR *without reproof, just information.*)
    She blew it.
    (*He goes out through the lobby doors.* BLAIR *takes a radio from*
    his pocket. The scene begins to change.)
BLAIR: (*To* RADIO) Ridley.
RIDLEY: (*On* RADIO) Ridley.
BLAIR: (*To* RADIO) I want Kerner in Regent's Park, twelve
    o'clock sharp.
    (*He puts the radio away and looks at his wrist-watch. The next*
    time he moves, it is twelve o'clock and he is at the zoo.)

SCENE 2

KERNER *has been brought by* RIDLEY *to the zoo.* BLAIR, *having*
checked the time on his watch, nods at RIDLEY *to dismiss him.*
RIDLEY *moves out.*
Perhaps we are looking at BLAIR *and* KERNER *through the bars of*
a cage. There could be a bench, there could be paper cups of coffee
. . . The bars make hard-edged shadows. We need one particular
and distinct demarcation of light and shadow on the floor, perhaps
thrown by the edge of a wall.
KERNER *speaks with a Russian accent, which is not too heavy; in*
fact, attractive.

BLAIR: You're blown, Joseph.
KERNER: I love it. She blew it and I'm blown: well, I'll be
    blowed. Nobody teaches that, you know. They teach you
    so you can almost read *David Copperfield* and then you find
    out that David is a language student too, he must have
    been put in as a sleeper.

BLAIR: Well . . . you're blowed, Joseph. Your career is over.

KERNER: Except as a scientist, you mean.

BLAIR: Yes, that's what I mean.

KERNER: My career as a joe.

BLAIR: Or as a sleeper. Just an observation. The meet at the pool came unstuck this morning. We have to consider you blown as our joe. The Russians must consider you blown as their sleeper. Either way your career is over. *Which* way, is perhaps an academic question.

KERNER: And yet, here you are.

BLAIR: One likes to know what's what.

KERNER: Oh yes! Objective reality.

BLAIR: I thought you chaps believed in that.

KERNER: 'You chaps'? Oh, *scientists*. (*Laughs*) 'You chaps!' Paul, objective reality is for zoologists. 'Ah, yes, definitely a giraffe.' But a double agent is not like a giraffe. A double agent is more like a trick of the light. Look. Look at the edge of the shadow. It is straight like the edge of the wall that makes it. Your Isaac Newton saw this and he concluded that light was made of little particles. Other people said light is a wave but Isaac Newton said, no, if light was a wave the shadow would bend round the wall like water bends round a stone in the river. Now we will do an experiment together.

BLAIR: *Now*, Joseph?

KERNER: Absolutely, In this experiment you have a machine-gun which shoots particles . . . which we call . . . ?

BLAIR: (*Tentatively*) Bullets?

KERNER: Bullets. You are shooting at a screen, say like a cinema screen. But between you and the screen I have put a wall of armour plate, so of course none of the bullets get through. Now I open two slits in the armour plate. (*He gestures to indicate the two slits a few inches apart.*) Now you shoot many times. Now you stop shooting and examine the screen and naturally it has bullet holes where some of the bullets came through the two slits. Opposite each slit there is a concentration of bullet holes, and maybe just a few holes to left and right from ricochets. This is called particle pattern. If your gun was a torch and light was bullets, as Isaac Newton said, this is what you will get. But when you do it you don't get it. You don't get particle pattern. You get wave pattern. Wave pattern is like stripes – bright, dim, bright, dim, across the screen. This is because when a wave is pushed through a little gap it spreads out in a semi-circle, so when you have *two* gaps you have two semi-circles spreading out, and on their way to the screen they mix together – so now you understand everything, yes? – no, you understand nothing, OK: where a crest from one lot of waves meets a crest from the other lot of waves you get a specially *big* wave, and where a crest meets a dip, the wave is cancelled out – strong, weak, strong, weak, on the screen it looks like stripes.

BLAIR: Joseph – I want to know if you're ours or theirs, that's all.

KERNER: I'm telling you but you're not listening. So, now light was waves, Isaac Newton was wrong about the bullets. But when light was waves there came a problem with a thing called the photo-electric effect, a real puzzle, which I will describe in detail with historical footnotes – OK, it was just to see your face. But this puzzle was a puzzle because everyone knew that light was waves. Einstein solved it. Or rather, he showed that if light was bullets after all, there was no puzzle. But how to explain the stripes on the screen, the wave pattern? Wave pattern happens when light from two slits mixes together but your particles can't do that – your bullet of light has already hit the screen before the next bullet is even fired. So there is only one solution.

BLAIR: What's that?

KERNER: Each bullet goes through both slits.

BLAIR: That's silly.

KERNER: Now we come to the exciting part. We will watch the bullets of light to see which way they go. This is not difficult, the apparatus is simple. So we look carefully and we see the bullets one at a time, and some hit the armour plate and bounce back, and some go through one slit, and some go through the other slit, and, of course, none go through both slits.

BLAIR: I knew that.

KERNER: You knew that. Now we come to my favourite bit. The wave pattern has disappeared! It has become particle pattern, just like with real machine-gun bullets.

BLAIR: Why?

KERNER: Because we looked. So, we do it again, exactly the same except now without looking to see which way the bullets go; and the wave pattern comes back. So we try again while looking, and we get particle pattern. Every time we don't look we get wave pattern. Every time we look to see how we get wave pattern, we get particle pattern. The act of observing determines the reality.

BLAIR: How?

KERNER: Nobody knows. Einstein didn't know. I don't know. There is no explanation in classical physics. Somehow light is particle and wave. The experimenter makes the choice. You get what you interrogate for. And you want to know if I'm a wave or a particle. I meet my Russian friend Georgi, and we exchange material. When the experiment is over, you have a result: I am a British joe with a Russian source. But they also have a result: because I have given Georgi enough information to keep him credible as a KGB control who is running me as a sleeper – *which is what he thinks he is.*

(*Pause.*)

BLAIR: It wasn't Georgi today.

KERNER: No?

BLAIR: No, it was different today.

KERNER: Today you decided to look. Why was that?

BLAIR: Some of your research has turned up in Moscow. Real secrets, not briefcase stuff.

KERNER: Tsk, tsk, tsk.

BLAIR: That's what the Americans said, roughly.

KERNER: The one shaving. He was American.

BLAIR: Mm. Ben Wates, CIA. You'd like him, he makes waves with a Smith and Wesson.

KERNER: I'm sorry, Paul.

BLAIR: (*Shrugs*) Cousin-trouble is nothing new. The other thing is trouble, though. Until this leak from Moscow the Russians were supposed to be locked into trying to match a space defence system which was going to drive them bonkers if it didn't drive them bankrupt first, while thanks to you our side was in quite another ballroom as Wates put it –

KERNER: Ballgame, I think.

BLAIR: I assure you it wasn't. Ballpark. Anyway, Wates flies in and says, 'I have come from Washington to help you. How about Kerner for a start? Do we know anything about Kerner?' Well, we do as a matter of fact. He's from Kaliningrad. The Russians put him in as a sleeper years ago but we turned him round and now he's really working for us, they only *think* he's working for them.

KERNER: What did he say?

BLAIR: He said: you guys.

KERNER: Poor Paul. What happened at the swimming pool?

BLAIR: Wates wanted us to pull the plug on it, close you down and send you to Sketchleys. But we thought we could show him you were clean while keeping the pool alive. We made Wates an offer. Mrs Hapgood and Ridley duplicated your delivery. They photographed all the documents again and made a copy of your computer disc. So now we had everything twice in two briefcases. Ridley took the second briefcase to the pool –

KERNER: What is Sketchleys?

BLAIR: I'm trying to tell you what happened at the pool.

KERNER: You already did. Ridley delivered to my Russian control. I delivered to Ridley. So, if I was adding anything to my briefcase, you get it all back.

BLAIR: That sort of thing. So Ridley intercepted your delivery and when we opened your briefcase Mrs Hapgood's films had gone.

KERNER: A puzzle.

BLAIR: Now we come to the exciting part. Wates had booby-trapped your briefcase. He sprayed the inside with an aerosol can, like radioactive deodorant – did you ever hear of such a thing?

KERNER: An isotope solution. If I open the briefcase I give a Geiger reading.

BLAIR: Yes, Wates shakes your hand and he has a counter which goes on the wrist and looks like a Rolex. We're working with people who tried to kill Castro with an exploding cigar. It's a joke shop. Wates also bugged your briefcase with a radio signal and tracked it to the pool. There it died and it might as well have gone to heaven. The bug disappeared. Nobody opened the briefcase. Wates has gone around shaking hands as though he were trying to get elected. Nobody gave a Geiger reading. The job was done by Mr Nobody. I feel sorry for Wates. All those belts and braces and now he can't find his trousers. *Our* trousers.

KERNER: Well I'm blown. Blow me for a monkey's uncle. Can I say that?

BLAIR: I would avoid it. By the way, do you know anything about twins?

KERNER: Twins?

BLAIR: That was the other thing. It wasn't Georgi today, it was twins.

(KERNER *laughs*.)

Yes, that's my favourite bit too. Give it some thought. Will you?

KERNER: Oh, yes. But excuse me, now it is time for the feeding of the seals.

(KERNER *strolls away, jerking his head at the unseen* RIDLEY *to follow him.* RIDLEY *re-enters and follows* KERNER *out at a comfortable distance.*

BLAIR *stands looking out front. The next time he moves he is on the touchline of a rugger pitch.*)

SCENE 3

BLAIR *is standing in an open exterior against a grey sky on a cold October afternoon. He is watching thirty eleven-year-old boys playing rugby. This, alas, is not as rich in sound effects as one might think: there is the referee's whistle, there are occasional piping exhortations to 'Heel', 'Drive', 'Shove', and so on, and the occasional sound of the ball being kicked, but much of all this is happening at a distance, and so the general effect is sporadic anyway. Nevertheless it would be nice to work out where* BLAIR *is before the next thing happens – which is that* HAPGOOD *comes hurtling crabwise and in full cry along the touchline. She is shod and dressed for the conditions and is carrying a boy's two-piece tracksuit, the top half of which is perhaps tied round her neck. Her momentum takes her a good way along the front of the stage, passing in front of* BLAIR.

HAPGOOD: Come on, big shove now, St Christopher's! Heel! –
　　break! . . . *well tackled*, darling! – I mean, Hapgood – oh,
　　sugar . . .
　　(*The match recedes but she always gives it as much attention as
　　she can spare or as she is allowed.*)
　　Look at their little knees. Don't you love little boys?
BLAIR: It's never been encouraged in the Service.
HAPGOOD: Well, don't look so cross about it.
BLAIR: I'm not cross.
HAPGOOD: Serious, then.
BLAIR: Yes, serious.
HAPGOOD: I know, Paul. I know it's serious. I'm awfully glad
　　to see you. How did you know where to find me?
BLAIR: Don't be silly. I know where you go when the sugar hits
　　the fan. Which one is he?
HAPGOOD: The handsome one with the nicest knees.
BLAIR: Oh, yes.
HAPGOOD: Don't wave.
BLAIR: I wasn't going to.
HAPGOOD: I waved once. He told everyone he was adopted.

You are nice wearing the scarf, you don't have to.

BLAIR: I like the scarf. I wanted to see you –

HAPGOOD: – wanted to see you –

BLAIR: – before you see Wates.

HAPGOOD: (*Turning back to the game*) Oh, yes.

BLAIR: It's Washington that's cross. They want – (*But she's off again*).

HAPGOOD: Kick! – kick for touch! – oh, sugar! – Tackle! – tackle low . . .

(*Referee's whistle. Bad news for* HAPGOOD.)

Oh . . . Bad luck, St Christopher's! Little darlings, they look so cold. Sixteen love.

BLAIR: Nil. Washington wants us to take Kerner off everything.

HAPGOOD: I know, Paul. I got an earful from Downing Street. What have the Americans got against Kerner?

BLAIR: Well, this is just an educated guess but I suppose if they're going to spend a few million dollars over here on Kerner's research programme they'd rather he didn't keep swapping briefcases with the men's freestyle champion of the Russian Embassy.

HAPGOOD: Paul, Kerner is my star.

BLAIR: Means nothing.

HAPGOOD: Do you want me to tell you or not? I had six month's work in Kerner's package – long-term reflectors on countdown –

BLAIR: (*Complaining*) Oh, Elizabeth, do talk English.

HAPGOOD: Well, in the next war some of the missiles carry warheads and some carry lots of milk-bottle tops to confuse the scanners – reflectors, all right? – disinformation that had to be launched, I couldn't *afford* to abort the meet just because Washington got into a flap about Kerner.

BLAIR: You can't blame Washington. When the Russians planted Kerner on us it was like laying down Cheval Blanc 'forty-seven, he's turned into pure gold, he's the man with the anti-particle trap, whatever that may be and I don't want you to tell me, but if he's leaking his own stuff to

Moscow we're making it awfully easy for him.

HAPGOOD: Kerner's all right – I run him and he's just doing what I tell him.

BLAIR: Wates made the same point. Don't take it personally.

HAPGOOD: Why would I? It isn't personal.

(*The referee's whistle – the conversion of the try.*)

Eighteen. Come on, St Christopher's! Let's get one back! This is personal, all fifteen of them and the referee, who's incidentally a sweetheart, he takes Divinity and says if Joe passes Common Entrance it'll make the loaves and fishes look like a card trick. Everything else is technical. You're personal sometimes; but not this minute which is all right, so what can I tell you? – it isn't Kerner.

BLAIR: So what *can* you tell me, Elizabeth?

All right, what happened at the pool? It's a technical question, it almost looks as if you could solve it with pencil and paper: cubicles A, B, C, D, briefcases P, Q, R, find X when the angles are Kerner and the Russian twins, which is a question in itself – are these the famous KGB twins? Now that's what I call a double agent. Who's in charge and is he sane?

HAPGOOD: I hate it, Paul.

BLAIR: Yes, why aren't we pleased?

HAPGOOD: It reeks. Those damned twins are like an old joke which keeps coming back, I've been hearing it for years and I never believed it. And suddenly here they are, identical and large as life. I hate it.

BLAIR: Do you want to keep them for a while?

HAPGOOD: No – chuck 'em out. They're stooges, Paul. The meet this morning went exactly as the Russians planned it, including the arrests. The twins weren't necessary, there must be another reason for them. They were meant to be seen, they were a success – 'Now he's here, now he's there, oh my God, there's two of them' – Wates nearly cut himself shaving he was so fascinated. He's done a diagram, on pink paper, showing who was where when, all the coming and going.

BLAIR: And?

HAPGOOD: Guess who was holding the briefcase when the bug went off the air.

BLAIR: Who was?

HAPGOOD: I was.

(*Referee's whistle – a try is scored.*)

BLAIR: Twenty-two nil. Our side isn't doing too well. Well, if it's you I don't care which side traps its particles. Anti-particles. Do you know what they are? They were never mentioned by Democritus who was the pro-particle chap when I was at school. Tell me what you know, Elizabeth.

HAPGOOD: (*Deflecting*) There's not a lot to them but when a particle meets an anti-particle they annihilate each other, they turn into energy – bang, you understand. Unfortunately anti-matter doesn't hang around, you can produce anti-particles in a collider and bottle them in a magnetic field but then you're stuck – the bottle is as big as a barn, and when you open the door you've got a billionth of a second so you have to be quick. If you could slow them down enough to get hold of you'd be in business, and Kerner thinks he can. Do you want me to tell you how?

BLAIR: No, don't bother.

HAPGOOD: (*Shouts*) Break! Blind!

BLAIR: I gave a chap a job with us once because he said he'd read physics and I thought he meant the book by Aristotle.

HAPGOOD: Was that last try converted?

BLAIR: No.

HAPGOOD: You weren't looking.

BLAIR: They re-started with a drop-kick.

HAPGOOD: Well, they're ten years away from anything like a weapon. Joe will be twenty-one. I'll be forty-eight. You'll be about a hundred. He's worried about something too, we've both got the same look.

BLAIR: His won't be anything serious.

HAPGOOD: Everything is serious. He got unhappy about something once when he was really little, he was crying, he couldn't tell me what it was, he didn't *know* what it was,

and he said, 'The thing is, Mummy, I've been unhappy for
years'. He was only as big as a gumboot.

(*She takes his arm for a moment.*)

Now he won't look. He's disgusted by extravagant displays
of affection on the touchline.

BLAIR: I've lost him again – you can't tell one from the other
when they're all in the same get-up.

HAPGOOD: (*Turning to* BLAIR) That's right! – you're nearly
there. I got it just before half-time. I don't know what it
means, please tell me it means nothing. Paul, brace
yourself. Ridley's by the pool, Ridley's Russian is getting
dressed. Merryweather's Russian arrives. Merryweather
follows his Russian in and he follows the other Russian out,
and why not? – they're identical and he only saw them one
at a time, it could happen to anybody, especially to
Merryweather, bless him, he probably still doesn't know
there were two of them. Now Ridley comes from the pool
and the same thing happens to him. He followed one
Russian in and he follows the other one out, and why not?
– they're identical and he only saw them one at a time.
Then he comes back inside and he says, 'You didn't tell me
it was twins.'

(*Referee's whistle, a longer one indicating the end of the game.*)
It's true, I didn't.

(*Distantly the two rugby teams call for three cheers for each
other, first for St Christopher's, secondly for St Codron's.*)

BLAIR: So how did he know?

HAPGOOD: He was expecting twins. I think it's Ridley, Paul.
I've left my own back door open.

(*Clapping*) Well played, St Christopher's . . . bad luck –

BLAIR: Oh, f-f-fiddle!

(JOE *enters.*)

HAPGOOD: Hello, darling.

JOE: Hello, Mum.

(*He is very muddy and glad to see her. His boots are a size too
large.*)

HAPGOOD: Bad luck – well played anyway. Put this on.

JOE: Thanks.

> (*He takes the tracksuit and puts it on.* HAPGOOD *helps him a little.*)

BLAIR: Hello, Joe. I'm afraid they were rather good, weren't they?

JOE: Yess'a.

BLAIR: How are you otherwise?

JOE: All rights'a, thank-yous'a. We always get beaten. I wish you wouldn't watch, Mum.

HAPGOOD: Well, I like watching, I don't mind if you get beaten.

JOE: But nobody watches except you.

HAPGOOD: There's lots of people watching – look over there.

JOE: That's the *firsts* – that's what I *mean*, nobody watches Junior Colts B – !

HAPGOOD: I do.

JOE: I *know*, Mum –

HAPGOOD: Well, I won't, then.

JOE: I like you *coming* –

HAPGOOD: I didn't shout this time –

JOE: You did a bit, Mum.

HAPGOOD: Hardly at all, whose boots are those?

JOE: Mine.

HAPGOOD: No, they're not.

JOE: Yes they are, I bought them.

HAPGOOD: Where?

JOE: From Sandilands.

HAPGOOD: Who's Sandilands?

JOE: He's had his kidney out so he does computers.

HAPGOOD: Oh. How much?

JOE: A pound.

HAPGOOD: A pound? What was wrong with yours?

JOE: I lost one.

HAPGOOD: You lost a rugby boot?

JOE: Yes. Well, not exactly, I mean I haven't *got* any rugger boots.

HAPGOOD: (*Irked*) Of course you have, what were you playing in before?

JOE: My hockey shoes – it doesn't matter, nobody minds –

HAPGOOD: You mean you *never* had any rugby boots?

JOE: Only this term, Mother –

HAPGOOD: Why didn't you say? – those look too big anyway, how old is Sandilands?

JOE: *It's all right*, it's silly to buy new boots for Colts B.

HAPGOOD: And now you've lost a hockey shoe? How did that happen?

JOE: It's not lost, it's on the roof.

HAPGOOD: I don't wish to know about this.

JOE: I borrowed the key for Mr Clark's garage where there's the ladder, I was going to get it down in break with the ladder but then I lost it.

HAPGOOD: You lost the ladder?

JOE: No, *the key*, Mum – I put it somewhere and Mr Clark will have an epi if I don't find it.

HAPGOOD: Is that what you're worried about, Mr Clark's garage key?

BLAIR: I'll send one of the burglars.

JOE: It's all right, don't *do* anything, Mum –

HAPGOOD: I won't. When was all this?

JOE: Today after breakfast – oh: thank you for the parcel. Your card came too. When were you in Austria? Did you go to the Spanish horses?

HAPGOOD: No, I was too busy. What was in the parcel?

JOE: The chocolate animals.

HAPGOOD: Oh, yes.

JOE: I gave one to Roger.

HAPGOOD: How is Roger?

JOE: I think he's pregnant.

HAPGOOD: Oh dear.

JOE: Well, he's awfully fat and he only eats chocolate.

HAPGOOD: Oh, well . . .

JOE: I've got to go –

HAPGOOD: Yes, don't miss tea – have you told **Mr Clark** you've lost his garage key?

JOE: No, I mean, he doesn't know I borrowed it.

HAPGOOD: Don't tell him yet – do the grid for me. From getting up, to when you couldn't find it. You remember how we do that?

JOE: It's all right, Mother –

HAPGOOD: I know it's all right. Just do the grid – five minutes for every square, don't leave any out because the key is in one of them, and phone me in first break if you haven't found it.

JOE: Yes, all right, thanks, Mum – thanks for coming –

BLAIR: Goodbye, Joe.

JOE: Goodbyes'a.

HAPGOOD: Bye, darling – I'll let you know when I can come again –

(*They exchange a kiss and he runs off.*)

BLAIR: (*Suddenly hearty*) I say – what a jolly nice young chap! Splendid –

HAPGOOD: (*Affectionately*) Oh, don't, Paul – I'm all right about *him* but if you start being good at children I'll cry, it's like those chimps being good at pouring tea, they try so hard . . .

BLAIR: This is most unfair. Excellent knees, I was thinking. You know, you should go to the Spanish Riding School some time when you're next in Vienna – really worth it.

HAPGOOD: (*Tightly*) Right, fine, thanks, point taken – I sent him a postcard; sorry. Oh, *sugar*, Paul!

BLAIR: I merely said –

HAPGOOD: No, you're right, I break the rules, and if Matron is KGB it's going to be all over Dzerzhinsky Square – Hapgood was in Vienna. Well, I keep *missing* things, last time I missed him in *Robin Hood* even if he *was* only a tree, and if I can't send him a rotten postcard you can take Vienna and stick it up your –

BLAIR: Right, fair enough –

HAPGOOD: – jumper! Oh, fiddle – what's he doing in a boarding school anyway?

BLAIR: Take him out.

HAPGOOD: To live with whom? He'd have to put himself to bed
four times a week even when I'm working out of Half
Moon Street – I already run the only intelligence network
in the Western world which exhibits seasonal fluctuations,
and it's only a matter of time before somebody works out
it's the school holidays. Anyway, there's the male society
thing, they're supposed to need that when they haven't got
fathers. Really I should pack it in.

BLAIR: Joe would be here just the same. You approve.

HAPGOOD: Yes, probably. I like all that manners maketh man
stuff, and competition and talking properly and being
magnanimous in victory and defeat – middle-class values,
I'm in favour and I'm not going to chuck them because
they happen to be shared by a fair number of people you
wouldn't want to be seen dead with, they always were. Are
we going to talk about me or Ridley?

BLAIR: Oh, yes, Ridley. You could be right about him. It
makes one wonder about that Bulgarian we lost in
Paris . . .

HAPGOOD: Ganchev, I thought so too. And Athens.

BLAIR: Yes, Athens. Wates will like that one.

HAPGOOD: It's a mess.

BLAIR: Yes. Frankly I'd rather it were Kerner. That's just a
better mousetrap. The real secrets are about intentions and
deployment, and Ridley could make it shit city around
here, I like the way they talk, the Americans, don't you –
so direct, descriptive, demotic – no, of course you don't –
do you never use bad language, never ever? What do you
say when you burn your hand on a saucepan? 'Oh, sugar'?

HAPGOOD: I don't cook.

BLAIR: I didn't know you knew. Well, what are we going to do
about Ridley? We could reel him in for a hostile interview
but that would only alter the degree of probability, I'd
rather catch him at it.

HAPGOOD: Yes, that's right. We missed our chance today, we'll
have to make him do it all again.

BLAIR: (*Surprised*) He won't come back to the well, it's been poisoned.

HAPGOOD: I know. It's difficult. I'll think about it. Do you want some tea? They lay it on for parents and he's entitled to two.

BLAIR: (*Shakes his head*) I think I'd better get the search going in back numbers. Perhaps you could organize a relief team from eight o'clock.

HAPGOOD: I've done that.

BLAIR: And someone should tell Downing Street we're standing by Kerner.

HAPGOOD: I've done that too.

BLAIR: Well . . . (*He nods goodbye at her.*) Don't pack it in yet, I need you.

HAPGOOD: I suppose that's technical, is it?

BLAIR: I suppose so.

HAPGOOD: Just making sure. I was calling you at the pool this morning. Where were you?

BLAIR: I was there.

HAPGOOD: I needed *you*.

BLAIR: No, no, that was only personal. But you're going to need me now.

HAPGOOD: I'll see you tomorrow. I'll be twenty minutes late in, there's something I have to do.

(BLAIR *watches her go. The next time he moves he's in Hapgood's office giving his hat to* MAGGS *and taking off his overcoat.*)

SCENE 4

Hapgood's office, ten a.m.
There is a door from MAGGS's *office. A window would be nice but is not necessary. There is a desk with the usual stuff including at least two telephones one of which is red. Push-button dialling. You can dial without picking up the receiver, and you can talk to* MAGGS *without picking up anything. There is a photograph frame on the desk, not too large. There is a safe. There is a decent old polished table big enough for six people to meet though we never need it for*

*more than four. It might be nice to make the conference table and the
desk all one thing so long as* HAPGOOD *doesn't look like Mussolini
at work. An armchair would be useful but not if it has to be carried
on. Anyway, there should be room to walk around.* MAGGS *is
Hapgood's secretary. He is young, calm, professional.*

MAGGS: Mrs Hapgood will be late. I've told Mr Wates.
BLAIR: Is he here? I didn't see him.
MAGGS: He's washing his hands and can he have a word.
BLAIR: Well, I'm here.
MAGGS: He said to say he's washing his hands and can he have
    a word.
BLAIR: Don't be silly.
MAGGS: That's what he said. Can I get you some tea?
BLAIR: No, I don't think so, thank you, I had some. Was that
    Merryweather out there?
MAGGS: Yes, sir.
BLAIR: Well, somebody should go and tell Mr Wates to stop
    washing his hands.
MAGGS: I'll ask Mr Merryweather.
    (MAGGS *takes* BLAIR's *hat and coat and scarf out.*
    Under the coat BLAIR *looks a bit rumpled, yesterday's shirt,
    that sort of feeling. He has a* Daily Telegraph. *He makes
    himself comfortable and opens it up.*
    The red telephone rings. It has its own sound. BLAIR *takes no
    notice.*
    MAGGS *hurries in.)*
BLAIR: It's the red line, I thought I wouldn't get in the way.
MAGGS: (*Into phone*) Mrs Hapgood's office . . . oh, hello, – I'm
    sorry she isn't in . . . Yes, I'm fine, thanks, how are things
    your end?
    (WATES *enters, looking terrific: suit, white shirt, tie, polished
    shoes. The clothes are loose enough for the gun and the radio to
    be in there somewhere but not baggy.*
    BLAIR *gets up to greet him.)*
BLAIR: Ben! Good morning!
WATES: Paul.

BLAIR: Come in – sit down –

MAGGS: (*Into phone*) . . . Uh, hold on a moment –

BLAIR: Mrs Hapgood won't be long.

MAGGS: (*To* BLAIR) Excuse me – should I . . . ?

BLAIR: No, no – it's perfectly all right. (*To* WATES) Downing Street.

WATES: Uh-huh.

MAGGS: (*Into phone*) Oh, I see – well, I can write down the grid for you . . .

BLAIR: (*Hastily*) The *Telegraph* has got a lot better, I notice . . . doesn't come off on your hands the way it used to. Maggs said you were washing your hands, but he didn't say of what.

WATES: You guys.

BLAIR: (*Cheerfully*) Yes, it's wit city around here.

WATES: No, you're funny like funny money, it doesn't mean everything it says.

MAGGS: (*Into phone*) He threw your boot on the roof.

WATES: I'm not listening.

MAGGS: (*Into phone*) Uh-huh. One square finding Whitaker for Matron. In the toilet, all right – two squares just dossing about, all right –

WATES: What number Downing Street?

MAGGS: (*Into phone*) Oh! Have you got another 10p?

BLAIR: (*To* WATES) Eleven.

MAGGS: (*Into phone*) I'll call you straight back from my office. (*He puts down the red phone and leaves, closing the door.*)

BLAIR: You wanted a word, I think . . .

WATES: Well . . .

BLAIR: . . . in the washroom.

WATES: (*Apologizing*) It's a kind of compliment.

BLAIR: No, no, I understand, I was only surprised that after recent experience you still thought Mrs Hapgood would be deterred from joining us in the men's lavatory.

(WATES *gets up, or perhaps he hasn't sat down, his manner is restless. He considers the red telephone, perhaps touches it gently. He takes in the photo frame, without touching it.*)

26

WATES: (*Quietly*) Mother.

BLAIR: Mm?

WATES: Ridley and the other one, Merryweather, they call her Mother.

BLAIR: Yes.

WATES: There's a son.

BLAIR: There is a son but she was called Mother when she joined the Defence Liaison Committee – the tea would arrive and the Minister would say, 'Who's going to be mother?'

WATES: She was the only woman.

BLAIR: Yes. She's still the only woman.

WATES: Is there a Mr Hapgood?

BLAIR: No.

WATES: Dead?

BLAIR: Is this idle curiosity?

WATES: You tell *me*.

BLAIR: Hapgood is her own name. Mrs is a courtesy title. It saves a lot of explanation. Usually.

WATES: Do you mind if I ask you something, Paul?

BLAIR: I'm beginning to.

(WATES, *deflected, moves back to the desk and this time picks up the photo frame and looks at it.*)

WATES: It's a funny thing, when I was the first black man to make it to the seventh floor at Langley, nobody ever asked me to pour them their tea. (*He puts the frame carefully back on the desk. Suddenly impatient*) Look, it's simple: do you know who the kid's father is or not?

(BLAIR *stares back at him, quite blank, and* WATES *lets it go.* WATES *has a complaint now.*)

She calls me Wates.

BLAIR: It's a sort of compliment.

WATES: It doesn't sound friendly.

BLAIR: Mister wouldn't be friendly.

WATES: You call me Ben.

BLAIR: That's another sort of compliment.

WATES: *She* doesn't call me Ben.

27

BLAIR: That would be friendly but not necessarily a
  compliment.

WATES: She calls you Paul.

BLAIR: Yes, but we're friends.

WATES: Can you explain this in some way I'd understand it?
  (BLAIR *considers the question.*)

BLAIR: No, I don't think so.

WATES: You guys.

BLAIR: What did you want to talk about?

WATES: Ridley.

BLAIR: All right.

WATES: You don't look surprised.

BLAIR: It's deceptive.

WATES: I was thinking about Ridley. Kerner delivers but
  Ridley intercepts. Ridley intercepts and delivers to
  Hapgood. Ridley and Hapgood. Hapgood and Ridley. I
  know the tune. You didn't tell me it was him in Athens.

BLAIR: Oh, yes, Athens.

WATES: Talk to me about Athens, Paul, since we're friends.

BLAIR: Well, there was a radio operator in the Russian Embassy
  in Athens who was cheating on his wife with a local girl we
  put in his way, which made him a soft target. Mrs
  Hapgood came out from London to look him over. Ridley
  was at that time number three in the Athens station.
  Between them they turned him round, a straight blackmail
  job but it went wrong and as you know we had to pull
  Ridley out of Athens in a hurry.

WATES: He killed an American agent.

BLAIR: That isn't how I'd put it.

WATES: How would you put it?

BLAIR: It was a sideshow. The girl was doing a little dealing in
  cocaine and she got raided by the local drugs squad –
  simply bad luck, but her pimp took it into his head that
  Ridley had set her up. He tried to shoot Ridley on the
  stairs of his apartment and Ridley shot him first. The fact
  that the pimp turned out to be on the Company pay-roll
  doesn't make him an American agent in my book, he was

28

    still a pimp and he was trying to kill one of my people.

WATES: The girl was busted while your Russian was in her flat.

BLAIR: Yes, most unfortunate.

WATES: You mean for him.

BLAIR: Also for him.

WATES: Flown back to Moscow in a sick-bag.

BLAIR: Yes.

WATES: Look at the score. One American source dead, one Russian target blown, one honeytrap busted – that's three nothing to them, and Ridley moves on to Paris. (*Pause.*) Now I'm thinking about Ganchev, you remember Ganchev?

BLAIR: Ganchev. I can't quite place him.

WATES: Bulgarian. He was one of your joes, shot dead in Paris. He was your Bulgarian – he got blown – the Bulgarians took him out – boom! – and you can't quite place him.

BLAIR: Oh, yes, Ganchev.

WATES: Right, Miron Ganchev. He was Ridley's joe, wasn't he?

BLAIR: Yes, that's right.

WATES: He was making a meet with Ridley and he was killed opening the door of a safe house in the rue Velásquez except it wasn't a safe house any more.

BLAIR: Yes.

WATES: It was Ridley's meet. Two doorkeys, whoever gets there first waits for whoever gets there second. Ridley was second.

BLAIR: Yes.

WATES: Ganchev didn't need to open the door unless he put the chain on, and he wouldn't take the chain *off* unless he liked what he saw through the spy-hole.

BLAIR: I think I can see what you're getting at but unfortunately Ganchev was shot at a range of about nine inches and Ridley was in a taxi in a traffic jam on the wrong side of the river. We went into it.

WATES: No, you don't see. Who says he was in a taxi? (*Pause.*)

BLAIR: (*Quietly*) Ben, I really wouldn't want you to make an ass of yourself.

WATES: Who says he was in a taxi?

BLAIR: Fuck off.

WATES: It was Hapgood. She was in the taxi too. Ganchev
wanted to talk to someone from London. And you went
into it. Did you get the taxi driver? No. You had Ridley's
boss.

BLAIR: (*Flares up*) What is this – couldn't you sleep? This is
stood on *nothing*: if Ridley did it, Hapgood must have
alibi'd him: if Hapgood alibi'd him Ridley must have done
it. You've got nothing, Ben, except insomnia.

WATES: That's what it was. Nine p.m. Washington time I'm in
Grosvenor Square, I'm going through the whole thing
again, I'm thinking about the radio signal in Kerner's
briefcase. It gets to the meet, no question. Kerner delivers,
Ridley collects, Ridley delivers, Hapgood collects. The
signal goes dead.

BLAIR: It's still insomnia.

WATES: (*Imperturbably*) It's still insomnia and I'm still thinking
about Kerner's bleep. It went off the air but what does that
mean? Maybe it went off the air, maybe we lost the
frequency, maybe it hopped frequencies, maybe there was
an override, you know what I mean? I didn't believe any of
it, I just wanted to get rid of these things so I could forget
the bleep and think about something else. So my guy's
radio-finder is sitting on the desk and I put on the phones
and I tune it in . . . and, Paul, it was alive. It was
transmitting like a bullfrog.

BLAIR: Three o'clock in the morning?

WATES: (*Nods.*) I start waking people up. I have a vector on it,
I need co-ordinates, I need a mobile. By four o'clock I
know which street, I know the building, I know which
corner of the building, I know how high up the building
within eight feet, I mean, shit, I know which *room*. It was
coming from this office. The bleep has come back home.
It's here.

BLAIR: Why didn't you wake me?

WATES: Where were you sleeping?
  (*Pause.*)
BLAIR: Where is she now?
WATES: You're asking me?
BLAIR: (*Snaps*) Yes, I'm asking you.
WATES: Excuse me. (*He takes the radio out of his coat. To*
  RADIO) Wates – who's in the Toyota?
RADIO: Collins, sir.
WATES: Where're you at?
RADIO: Half Moon Street. Target is home.
  (WATES *puts the radio back in his pocket.*)
WATES: She just walked in downstairs.
BLAIR: Good.
WATES: We should hold back a little, feel this thing out.
BLAIR: Don't worry. Incidentally, where did she go this
  morning?
WATES: Shopping.
BLAIR: Shopping.
WATES: As I say, it makes sense to hold back, Paul, give her a
  little room, you understand me?
BLAIR: Of course.
  (*The door opens and* HAPGOOD *enters briskly. She has her
  shopping with her. There is a Lillywhites' carrier bag and a
  little Fortnum's bag.*)
HAPGOOD: Good morning! – Paul – Wates –
BLAIR: Good morning! – Guess what – Kerner's bleep came
  alive in the night, it seems to be coming from your office.
WATES: Aw, shit.
HAPGOOD: Golly, Wates.
WATES: I meant golly.
HAPGOOD: Sit down.
WATES: I've been sitting, I like standing, ma'am.
  (MAGGS *enters. He comes from the outer office with stuff for*
  HAPGOOD's *attention; a wooden tray [shallow box]
  overflowing with open letters, memos, etc., and a separate lot of
  sensitive material which might even be in a little attaché case or
  a closable file. The tray is put on the desk; it's the other lot of*

stuff which HAPGOOD *looks through first.*)

MAGGS: Good morning. Do you want to see the decrypts?

(HAPGOOD *is behind her desk.* BLAIR *has sat down again where he was sitting, and* WATES *probably stays standing.* MAGGS *stands.*)

HAPGOOD: (*To* MAGGS) Thank you. Anything else?

MAGGS: Joe telephoned. I wrote down the grid.

HAPGOOD: Thank you – don't go. (*To* WATES) What time, Wates?

WATES: Two fifty – three o'clock . . .

HAPGOOD: Uh-huh.

(*She has scooped the decrypts, etc., out of their case.* MAGGS *gets the case.* HAPGOOD *starts going through the pile of stuff. There's not very much of it. But unless otherwise stated she is reading the material continuously, making notes on pages which one by one go back to* MAGGS *and back into the case. She reads while she listens and she also reads while she talks to* WATES. *But for* BLAIR *she looks up.*)

(*To* BLAIR) Did you see this from Bonn?

BLAIR: Mm.

HAPGOOD: I'll send someone in to help.

(*She scribbles and holds the page up to* MAGGS.)

BLAIR: If I were you I'd lift him out.

(*She checks, considers this, accepts it, rescribbles, hands the page to* MAGGS. *We have no idea what that's about and never will.*)

HAPGOOD: (*To* WATES) It was alive when you checked, so you don't know when it came on air.

WATES: That's right.

HAPGOOD: (*To* MAGGS) This one to Special Branch in the pouch. This one to the Russian Desk by hand.

(*To* WATES) And you got a triangulation and the beams crossed in this office.

WATES: Yes, ma'am.

HAPGOOD: Is it still giving out?

WATES: As far as I know.

HAPGOOD: And you would know, wouldn't you?

(*It is clear now that he is not popular with her this morning.*)
(*Icy*) Why didn't you call me?
(*He doesn't reply so she gives him a glance.*)
Understood. (*She bangs a few buttons on her telephone console and then lifts the handset.*)
(*Into phone.*) Get me the form on a white Toyota van VRY 434X Cornucopia Catering, Uxbridge phone number.

WATES: (*Pleading guilty*) Yeah, all right.

HAPGOOD: (*Into phone*) Cancel. (*She puts the phone down.*)
(*To* WATES) I'll get back to that. So did you bring a radio-finder with you? (*To* MAGGS) This one upstairs, this one reconfirm.

WATES: No, ma'am.

HAPGOOD: You thought you'd give me first crack. That's all right.

WATES: Ma'am, this is a 500 millisecond-repeat transponder-transmitter locked on seventeen megahertz with a lithium battery and a gate interrupter . . . it . . .
(*He falters because she appears to be absorbed in her next paper.*)

HAPGOOD: Interrupter.

WATES: It gives it a signature, it has to be the same bleep.

HAPGOOD: That's what I was wondering. (*She repeats the business with the phone console.*)
(*Into phone*) Get hold of the day book – everyone in or out of this building in the last twenty-four hours, but everyone . . . thank you.
(*She puts the phone down. She scribbles on the last decrypt, hands it to* MAGGS *and takes the top sheet off the other pile.*)
These transponders . . . it went dead at ten-oh-seven yesterday morning and it was alive again at three a.m. Can they come and go like that?

WATES: Not that I ever heard. My guy couldn't figure it either. They're either fixed or broke, they don't fix themselves. If they're quiet they're either dead or out of range, and if it got out of range it must have been taken there in a lead box.

HAPGOOD: Uh-huh. Did he mention a hamster?

WATES: A what?

HAPGOOD: (*To* MAGGS) Roger.

MAGGS: No.

HAPGOOD: You sure? – empty square before assembly –

MAGGS: No Roger-the-hamster.

HAPGOOD: Oh, the chump. (*Relieved*) That's all, Maggs. Tea.
(MAGGS *goes back to his office.* WATES *has had enough of this.*)

WATES: Excuse me – we don't need the day book – we don't
need to know where that baby's *been*, or how it got *away*,
or when it came *back*, it had no business coming back,
when I put on the phones I felt foolish like putting on a
stethoscope for a corpse that's been ten hours dead in the
water – but, ma'am, we've got a situation now and I'm glad
Paul is here because I'm asking him to ask you if you
would open up that safe you have there and then I won't
have to worry about it any more.
(HAPGOOD *has stopped listening. She sits thinking.*)
Paul?
(*He gets no help.* HAPGOOD *bangs the phone buttons and lifts
the receiver.*)

HAPGOOD: (*Into phone*) About the day book – cancel.
(*She puts the phone down. She gets up to go to the door but this
brings her close to* WATES.)
I could kiss you, Wates. (*She opens the door.*)
Merryweather. (*She heads back to her desk.*)

MERRYWEATHER: (*Entering*) Thanks, Mother, I don't need
long, it was just that I had a thought about our Russian
friend –

HAPGOOD: (*Sitting down*) In a minute. You drained the pool.

MERRYWEATHER: Yes, that's right.

HAPGOOD: How long did that take?

MERRYWEATHER: Ages – most of the day – right down to the
filter –

HAPGOOD: And?

MERRYWEATHER: Nothing much – hair grips – corn plasters
. . . there was a lens that looked interesting for a minute
but it was from a pair of goggles.

HAPGOOD: (*Impatiently*) Come on, come on –

MERRYWEATHER: It's all in there – I put it in Maggs's box last night –

(*He means a foolscap manila envelope in Maggs's pile.*
HAPGOOD *tears the envelope across, emptying the contents on to her desk, by which time –*)

HAPGOOD: Fat tiddlywink, like an aspirin –

MERRYWEATHER: Er, yes, that's right – a plastic counter –

(*Now she has found it among the corn plasters. She tosses it to* WATES *who catches it. Or perhaps she slides it down the table like a bartender.*)

HAPGOOD: Ten hours dead in the water. It only drowns the signal, when Merryweather fished it out it was back on the air.

(MAGGS *comes in with* HAPGOOD's *tea. It's like having tea at the Ritz without the sandwiches – nice china, tea pot, hot water jug, etc.*

BLAIR, *who has been sitting too still for too long, now stretches all the tension out of his body, sprawling in his chair, languid again.*)

BLAIR: I think I might change my mind about that tea, Maggs . . . how about you, Ben?

WATES: Yes. Thank you.

HAPGOOD: Just the cups, Maggs. Mr Wates takes it with lemon.

MAGGS: We haven't got a lemon.

HAPGOOD: Tsk, tsk, you must always keep a lemon.

MAGGS: (*Leaving*) The reply from Ottawa came in.

HAPGOOD: Oh yes?

MAGGS: Exchange bishops, and queen to king one.

HAPGOOD: Exchange bishops, my eye – he'll be lucky.

(MAGGS *leaves.* HAPGOOD *broods for a moment.*)

MERRYWEATHER: Mother . . .

HAPGOOD: Oh, I'm sorry, Merryweather –

MERRYWEATHER: It's just that I had a thought which may or may not be something.

HAPGOOD: Of course – tell us your thought.

MERRYWEATHER: Well, I was thinking about it and something

wasn't quite right. The Russian delivered to the changing
room and he came straight out again . . .

HAPGOOD: Yes?

MERRYWEATHER: He didn't have time for a swim or anything.

HAPGOOD: Uh-huh.

MERRYWEATHER: Well, this is the thing – I was thinking
about it and I'm pretty sure his towel was dry when I
followed him in but it was wet when I followed him out
. . . I was wondering if anybody had noticed that. (*Pause.*)
Well, it was just a thought I thought I'd leave with you.

HAPGOOD: It's a good thought, Merryweather, worth thinking
about. Thank you.

MERRYWEATHER: Fine. Any way I can help.

HAPGOOD: Actually, there's a job you can do for me.

MERRYWEATHER: Good – of course –

HAPGOOD: It's down the A30 past Staines.

MERRYWEATHER: Right. A meet?

HAPGOOD: A sort of meet. Just past Virginia Water you take a
right, the A329 to Bracknell, a couple of miles along there's
a prep school, St Christopher's.

(*From the Lillywhites' bag she produces a shoe box and gives
that to* MERRYWEATHER.)

Get there at exactly one fifty. You'll find a lot of small boys
charging around outside. Stop the first boy you see and say,
'Do you know Hapgood?'

MERRYWEATHER: 'Do you know Hapgood?'

HAPGOOD: The boy will say, 'Yes, sir.' There's an outside
chance he'll say, 'I am Hapgood, sir,' but probably not.
Give him this, and say, 'I have a message from Mother.'

MERRYWEATHER: 'Do you know Hapgood? I have a message
from Mother.' Is this the message?

HAPGOOD: No, the message is, 'The garage key is on Roger's
hutch.'

MERRYWEATHER: 'The garage key is on Roger's hutch.'

(MAGGS *comes in with the cups. He goes to add them to the
tray*.)

HAPGOOD: St Christopher's – the Bracknell road – one fifty.

MERRYWEATHER: Right. 'The garage key is on Roger's hutch.'

HAPGOOD: Thank you very much, Merryweather.

(*She has helped him out of the door.* MAGGS *is following* MERRYWEATHER *out.*)

(*To* MAGGS) Pawn to rook four, and tell him to put his queen back.

MAGGS: (*Continuing out*) Pawn to rook four.

(MAGGS *closes the door behind him. Pause.* WATES *has taken a sheet of pink paper from his pocket – a diagram. He folds it up now and places it on Hapgood's desk.*)

WATES: It's Ridley.

BLAIR: Mm.

WATES: I'm sorry. (*He is commiserating, not apologizing.*) You'll have to turn over everything he ever touched.

HAPGOOD: We're already doing that.

WATES: (*Surprised, wrong-footed*) Since when?

HAPGOOD: Since yesterday.

(*She flicks her thumb along* BLAIR's *jaw bone, a technical gesture.*)

You look awful. You only had to get the search going, not stay all night.

(*That's* WATES *wrong-footed twice.*)

(*To* WATES) Do you remember Ganchev, our Bulgarian? – Paul and I think that's one which needs looking at, did he tell you?

(*That's three times. He is suddenly really angry and the next four exchanges are a quick violent row.*)

WATES: You guys!

HAPGOOD: Wates –

WATES: My friends call me Ben!

HAPGOOD: I don't care what your friends call you, I want to tell you something – I will not be tagged by your people in my own *town*! You had two mobiles and a team of seven playing pass-the-parcel, I took them all round Lillywhites and I can number them off, don't think I can't, I've been followed by marching bands that did it better, and if they're not pulled by the time I go to lunch you're off the

37

bus. Is that entirely clear?

WATES: It's clear.

HAPGOOD: Good. Did they tell you I popped into Fortnum's?
(*From the little Fortnum's bag she takes a lemon, which is all the bag contains and adds it to the tea-tray.*)

HAPGOOD: Where are we, Paul?
(*She stabs the intercom button with her finger.*)
(*To intercom*) Maggs, you should have had a briefcase coming home on the van.

MAGGS: (*On intercom*) Yes, Mrs Hapgood.

HAPGOOD: I want it. (*She takes her finger away.*)

BLAIR: Where we are is that when the bug died it was no longer in the briefcase, it was in the water and Ridley was by the pool. We're no further than that.
(MAGGS *enters with the briefcase.*)

HAPGOOD: (*Taking it*) Thank you.
(MAGGS *goes out.*)
This is the dummy, retrieved from Tweedledum.
(*She puts the briefcase on the desk and opens it.* BLAIR *approaches and exhibits the contents of the briefcase.*)

BLAIR: One duplicate disc . . . five rolls of film . . .
(*The rolls of film are in a cloth bag.*
Meanwhile HAPGOOD *has taken an identical briefcase from the safe. She opens it for* BLAIR. *It contains only the disc, seen at the pool.*)

HAPGOOD: This is the original – Kerner's delivery.

BLAIR: (*To* WATES) Where did you plant Kerner's bleep?

WATES: In Kerner's bag of films.

BLAIR: Which Ridley removed. Why would he do that? He only had to take out what he put in and we'd be none the wiser.

WATES: Ridley put *in* a roll film, and they all look the same – he had to take them all.

HAPGOOD: Yes, that's nice.

WATES: Ma'am, it's beautiful, it's so beautiful it has to be right. The Russians put Kerner in place and they don't care if he's a double or a triple, they put him in as a channel for

38

Ridley. It's perfect. Packing Kerner's briefcase is Ridley's job. Kerner's job is delivering to the Russians. It's made in heaven. Yesterday it nearly came apart but only because of the leak from Moscow. The luggage was going to be inspected. Ridley had to get there first. He removed the films and handed you the briefcase in the shower. But now he had the bleep. He dropped it in the pool.

BLAIR: He did all that without opening the briefcase?

WATES: That's the bit I'm still working on. Your best chance is to make him do it all again.

HAPGOOD: That's right.

WATES: He left behind Kerner's disc. What's on it?

HAPGOOD: Reflectors. Raw data and some feedback from Geneva where Kerner's got beam-time on the CERN Proton Synchrotron.

WATES: Well, if Ridley has to come back for something, that's what you've got.

HAPGOOD: It's chickenfeed, we get the print-out cleared.

BLAIR: And Ridley knows it's chickenfeed.

WATES: He knows its chickenfeed because Kerner is your joe. Suppose Kerner was a sleeper.

HAPGOOD: That's good. Keep working.

WATES: If Kerner was double-crossing you, the disc wouldn't be chickenfeed. Say it's the jackpot, it's their ship coming in, and Ridley left it behind because he didn't know. He has to come back for it.

HAPGOOD: More.

WATES: Only Kerner hasn't got it. Hapgood has got it. Hapgood and Ridley, Ridley and Hapgood. There goes that song again. How are you at telling lies?

HAPGOOD: I make a living.

WATES: It's got to be you and him, like a team. Tell Ridley a good story, and you'll have him by the balls.

(*For* HAPGOOD) Excuse me.

HAPGOOD: Ben, you're welcome.

(*She turns her attention to the tea-tray.*)

(*brightly*) Well! Should I be mother?

SCENE 5

An indoor shooting range. But we don't really know that yet. We see
RIDLEY, *downstage in the only lit area, ready to shoot, holding his*
gun towards the dark upstage. RIDLEY *shoots six times. His shots*
are aimed at six illuminated targets which make their sudden and
successive appearances. Some of the targets are 'blue' and some
(most) are 'green'.*
No targets are showing when we see RIDLEY. *He starts shooting*
when the first target appears. RIDLEY's *six targets come up as four*
greens, then a blue, then a green. He hits the first two, misses the
third and fourth, hits the fifth, which is the blue, and the sixth.
RIDLEY's *conversation is with an amplified* VOICE. RIDLEY *doesn't*
have to raise his voice to reply, but his voice echoes.

VOICE: Stop shooting. Two misses, three greens and you killed
    a blue. Reload.
RIDLEY: Reloading.
VOICE: On your go, and remember blue is our side.
RIDLEY: Yes, sir.
    (HAPGOOD *enters quietly, walking behind* RIDLEY's *back.*)
VOICE: Mr Ridley, on your go.
RIDLEY: Go.
    (*The first target is blue.* RIDLEY *lets it live. The next five are*
    all green, rapid. RIDLEY *hits four, misses the fifth, and hardly*
    has time to curse before the target is knocked out by a sixth shot,
    from Hapgood's gun.)
VOICE: Wait a minute – wait a minute –
    (HAPGOOD *comes into* RIDLEY's *light, putting a small*
    automatic into her handbag.)
HAPGOOD: Hey, Ridley.
RIDLEY: Mother.
VOICE: Is that you, Mrs Hapgood?
HAPGOOD: (*Cheerful*) Hello, Mac. How've you been?

---

*Or, as in the first production, cut-out figures, of villains and civilians, with some
changes to the dialogue.

VOICE: Ma'am, you're breaking the rules.

HAPGOOD: I know, I'm hopeless. Will you give us the shop for a while?

VOICE: Do you want the mike?

HAPGOOD: No, no need.

VOICE: I'll be in the back.

HAPGOOD: Thank you.

(*We lose the echo.*)

(*To* RIDLEY) I have to talk to you.

RIDLEY: Funny place to choose.

HAPGOOD: I'm not sure that I want to be seen with you, Ridley.

(RIDLEY *considers this. He considers her. He has his gun in his hand. He puts the gun away behind him, into his waistband under his jacket next to his spine. He takes out a packet of cigarettes, puts one in his mouth, puts the packet away, and feels for the lighter.*)

HAPGOOD: Don't light it.

(RIDLEY *takes the cigarette out of his mouth and holds it unlit.*)

RIDLEY: What's the problem?

HAPGOOD: The problem is, someone's playing dirty and we're favourite.

RIDLEY: (*Quite pleased*) You and me? What have *we* done?

HAPGOOD: The story is we're bent. We've been using Kerner to pass real secrets. Yesterday it went wrong for us and we had to steal them back during the meet. You passed the briefcase to me and I emptied it.

RIDLEY: If this is Wates why doesn't he go for the obvious? The stuff was never in there.

HAPGOOD: Wates tracked it to the pool, he had a finder on the bleep. It stayed alive till the briefcase got to me.

(RIDLEY *laughs.*)

RIDLEY: I think I see. You cracked the transponder in your teeth.

HAPGOOD: I was in the shower. It doesn't work in water.

(RIDLEY *likes that even better.*)

RIDLEY: And what about the geiger? Didn't Wates shake your

hand?

HAPGOOD: Not till I'd opened the briefcase to see if we had a result, and I set him off like castanets. How do you like it so far?

RIDLEY: (*Delighted*) It's beautiful. I'm beginning to think you did it. I don't see that you'd need me.

HAPGOOD: Well, there are a couple of other things. Wates has been digging up the back garden and he thinks he's found some bones he can make bodies out of.

RIDLEY: Like what?

HAPGOOD: Like Athens.

RIDLEY: Ah, Athens. We *met* in Athens. Oh, Mother . . . Athens was the best time of my life.

HAPGOOD: Was it? We had an operation that blew up in our faces.

RIDLEY: What's that to Wates?

HAPGOOD: Well, the girl who was caught with the cocaine, she said you'd just left.

RIDLEY: That was rubbish.

HAPGOOD: I know – you were with me, in a parked car in Piraeus pretending to be lovers and waiting for our Russian who never turned up.

RIDLEY: How would I forget?

HAPGOOD: Don't leer, it suits you.

RIDLEY: What else?

HAPGOOD: Ganchev.

RIDLEY: Good heavens. What a team.

HAPGOOD: I tell you, Ridley, I'm sick of being your alibi. I can't blame Wates for wondering about us.

RIDLEY: Did Wates talk to you?

HAPGOOD: No.

RIDLEY: He talked to Paul Blair? Blair wouldn't be impressed. It's all circular. It can't be me without you, it can't be you without me, so it's both of us. Whatever happened to neither? Did Blair listen?

HAPGOOD: He listenened but he thinks he knows better.

RIDLEY: Trust, you see.

HAPGOOD: No, he just thinks it's Kerner.

RIDLEY: Yes, that makes sense.

HAPGOOD: Why?

RIDLEY: Every double is a possible triple – Blair would have to consider it.

HAPGOOD: Well, I hope he's wrong.

RIDLEY: That's a funny thing to say, Mother.

HAPGOOD: (*With passion*) *Kerner is my joe*! I turned him. If he's a triple, something must have turned him back again – recently, a few months . . .

RIDLEY: What would that be?

HAPGOOD: (*Shrugs*) *Toska po rodine.*

RIDLEY: What's that?

HAPGOOD: Homesickness, but squared. You have to be Russian.

RIDLEY: That could be. Did he leave a family?

HAPGOOD: Why?

RIDLEY: When I processed him after the meet I found a photograph, fingernail size, cut out with scissors, like from a team photo. It was hidden in the lining of his wallet, an amateur job . . . picture of a boy in a football shirt.

HAPGOOD: (*Looks at him steadily*) What did you do with it?

RIDLEY: I put it back, Mother. Do I have to keep calling you Mother? You can call me Ernest. (*Pause.*) Call me Ridley. (*He seems to be having trouble getting through to her.*) Listen, the whole meet was a blind. The goods were passed somewhere else. Kerner found the bug and put it in his pocket to keep us with him. Then he chucked it in the pool.

HAPGOOD: That's quite nice.

RIDLEY: Get the pool drained. You never know your luck.

HAPGOOD: Uh-huh. You're not bad, Ridley. The firm will miss you.

RIDLEY: Say again?

HAPGOOD: You're suspended. So am I. Wates took his story upstairs. Paul Blair is running my operations. Do you think I got you here for fun?

43

RIDLEY: God almighty. What do we do now?

HAPGOOD: You do what Blair tells you. In my office, seven o'clock, and you're there to listen, don't talk out of turn. By the way, we're not telling the Americans.

RIDLEY: Trust me. (*Then a flat challenge.*) Why don't you, as a matter of fact?

HAPGOOD: You're not safe, Ridley, You're cocky and I like prudence, you're street smart and this is a boardgame. In Paris you bounced around like Tigger, you thought it was cowboys and Indians. In Athens you killed a man and it was the best time of your life, you thought it was sexy. You're not my type. You're my alibi and I'm yours. Trust doesn't come into it.

RIDLEY: Well, go and fuck yourself, Hapgood, (*he now takes his lighter out and lights his cigarette with deliberate, insolent defiance*) since we're on suspension. You come on like you're running your joes from the senior common room and butter wouldn't melt in your pants but you operate like a circular saw, and you pulled me to watch your back because when this is a street business I'm your bloody type all right, and in Athens if you could have got your bodice up past your brain you would have screwed me and liked it.

(*He starts to leave.*)

HAPGOOD: Ridley.

(*He stops.*)

Safety.

RIDLEY: I didn't re-load.

HAPGOOD: You saved on the blue.

RIDLEY: That's true.

(*He takes his gun from the holster, checks it and puts it back.*)

Pity, really.

HAPGOOD: What is?

RIDLEY: I liked it when it was you and me. Ridley and Mother. It sounds like a firm of interior decorators.

(RIDLEY *leaves.*

KERNER *enters, coming towards her out of the dark and into the light. She sees him and is not surprised.*

44

She takes her radio out of her bag.)

HAPGOOD: (*To* RADIO) Is he clear?

RADIO: Green.

HAPGOOD: I'm here to be told.

(*She puts the radio back into her bag.*)

(*To* KERNER) Do you mean there's another one like him?

KERNER: Why not?

HAPGOOD: So where's the other one?

KERNER: Maybe that was the other one.

HAPGOOD: Joseph!

(*Their manner is as of intimate friends.*)

Did you look at Wates's drawing?

KERNER: (*Nods*) Positional geometry. Leibnitz. I'll tell you
about him.

HAPGOOD: No, don't.

KERNER: You're right, it's marginal. I'll tell you about
Leonhard Euler. Were you ever in Kaliningrad?

HAPGOOD: No, I'm afraid not.

KERNER: I was born in Kaliningrad. So was Immanuel Kant, as
a matter of fact. There is quite a nice statue of him. Of
course, it was not Kaliningrad then, it was Königsberg,
seat of the Archdukes of Prussia. President Truman gave
Königsberg to Stalin. My parents were not consulted and I
missed being German by a few months. Well, in Immanuel
Kant's Königsberg there were seven bridges. The river
Pregel, now Pregolya, divides around an island and then
divides again, imagine a pair of pincers with one bridge
across each of the handles and one across the hinge and
four bridges on to the island which would be the walnut if
you were cracking walnuts. An ancient amusement of the
people of Königsberg was to try to cross all the seven
bridges without crossing any of them twice. It looked
possible but nobody had solved it. Now, when Kant was
ten years old . . . what do you think?

HAPGOOD: Did he really? What a charming story.

KERNER: The little Kant had no idea either. No, when Kant
was ten years old, the Swiss mathematician Leonhard Euler

took up the problem of the seven bridges and he presented his solution to the St Petersburg Academy of Science in the form of a general principle based on vertices. Of course, Euler didn't waste his time walking around Königsberg, he only needed the geometry. (*He now produces Wates's diagram on pink paper.*) When I looked at Wates's diagram I saw that Euler had already done the proof. It was the bridges of Königsberg, only simpler.

HAPGOOD: What did Euler prove?

KERNER: It can't be done, you need two walkers.

(*Pause.*)

HAPGOOD: Good old Euler.

KERNER: You like it?

HAPGOOD: (*Nods*) It finally makes sense of Tweedledum and Tweedledee trailing their coats around the pool. A little while ago the Swedes got themselves a KGB defector and the famous twins turned up in his debriefing with a solid London connection. If two Ridleys are for real they must have felt the draught. Those two jokers at the meet were brought in as decoys. Reflectors. I never believed in the twins till then. I know about reflectors.

So who's in charge and is he sane?

KERNER: Has this place been dusted?

HAPGOOD: Dusted?

KERNER: We can talk?

HAPGOOD: (*Amused*) Oh, yes. We can talk. (*She regards him steadily.*) *Now* he's careful.

KERNER: The photograph? I'm ashamed.

HAPGOOD: (*Sudden force*) No, *I* am. Oh, fiddle!

KERNER: I mean, to be called an amateur.

HAPGOOD: Oh, Joseph.

KERNER: Yes, I'm one of your Joes. How is the little one?

HAPGOOD: He's all right. He's fine. Stop sending him chocolates, they're bad for his teeth and not good for his hamster.

Dusted is finger-prints, you know.

Microphones is swept. It really is disgraceful the way you

46

refuse to learn English.

KERNER: That's English? Where did you get *toska po rodine*?

HAPGOOD: From Nabokov.

KERNER: Where's he?

HAPGOOD: He's dead.

KERNER: He got caught?

HAPGOOD: (*Irritably*) No, Joseph, he's a writer.

KERNER: Oh – *Nabokov*. I only read spy stories.

HAPGOOD: It shows.

KERNER: I like them. Well, they're different, you know. Not from each other naturally. I read in hope but they all surprise in the same way. Ridley is not very nice: he'll turn out to be all right. Blair will be the traitor: the one you liked. This is how the author says, 'You see! Life is not like books, alas!' They're all like that. I don't mind. I love the language.

HAPGOOD: (*The language lover*) I'm awfully glad.

KERNER: Safe house, sleeper, cover, joe . . . I love it. When I have learned the language I will write my own book. The traitor will be the one you don't like very much, it will be a scandal. Also I will reveal him at the beginning. I don't understand this mania for surprises. If the author knows, it's rude not to tell. In science this is understood: what is interesting is to know what is happening. When I write an experiment I do not wish you to be *surprised*, it is not a *joke*. This is why a science paper is a beautiful thing: first, here is what we will find; now here is how we find it; here is the first puzzle, here is the answer, now we can move on. This is polite. We don't save up all the puzzles to make a triumph for the author – that is the dictatorship of the intelligentsia.

HAPGOOD: (*Insisting*) *Joseph* – twins.

KERNER: His name was Konstantin Belov, and, yes, he was sane, though in my opinion absurd.

HAPGOOD: More.

KERNER: He is not in charge now. The twins are his legacy.

HAPGOOD: You knew him?

KERNER: Sure. His training was particle physics. No original work and not much unoriginal. He got into State Security as some kind of researcher, then an instructor, then planner, then head of department; which is orbit. As head of department you have escaped from the pull of your ignorance, because now your colleagues are the heads of other departments, and however little you know about your subject they know even less; at that level you are the physicist. Now your problem is different – how to use your subject to make a path for yourself. One day Konstantin Belov jumped out of his bathtub and shouted, 'Eureka!' In Russian it means, 'Twins!' Maybe he shouted, 'By jiminy!'

HAPGOOD: You're mischievous.

KERNER: Maybe he was asleep in the bath. The particle world is the dream world of the intelligence officer. An electron can be here or there at the same moment. You can choose; it can go from here to there without going in between; it can pass through two doors at the same time, or from one door to another by a path which is there for all to see until someone looks, and then the act of looking has made it take a different path. Its movements cannot be anticipated because it has no reasons. It defeats surveillance because when you know what it's doing you can't be certain where it is, and when you know where it is you can't be certain what it's doing: Heisenberg's uncertainty principle; and this is not because you're not looking carefully enough, it is because there is *no such thing* as an electron with a definite position and a definite momentum; you fix one, you lose the other, and it's all done without tricks, it's the real world, it is awake.

HAPGOOD: Joseph, please explain to me about the twins.

KERNER: I just did but you missed it.

(*Pause.*)

HAPGOOD: So you did. It's crazy.

KERNER: (*Unmoved*) Oh, yes . . . but compared to the electron it is banal. Frankly, compared to the electron everything is banal. And the photon and the proton and the neutron . . .

Yelizaveta, when things get very small they get truly crazy, and you don't know how small things can be, you think you know but you don't know. I could put an atom into your hand for every second since the world began and you would have to squint to see the dot of atoms in your palm. So now make a fist, and if your fist is as big as the nucleus of one atom then the atom is as big as St Paul's, and if it happens to be a hydrogen atom then it has a single electron flitting about like a moth in the empty cathedral, now by the dome, now by the altar . . . Every atom is a cathedral. I cannot stand the pictures of atoms they put in schoolbooks, like a little solar system: Bohr's atom. Forget it. You can't make a picture of what Bohr proposed, an electron does not go round like a planet, it is like a moth which was there a moment ago, it gains or loses a quantum of energy and it jumps, and at the moment of the quantum jump it is like two moths, one to be here and one to stop being there; an electron is like twins, each one unique, a unique twin.

HAPGOOD: Its own alibi.

KERNER: It upset Einstein very much, you know, all that damned quantum jumping, it spoiled his idea of God, which I tell you frankly is the only idea of Einstein's I never understood. He believed in the same God as Newton, causality, nothing without a reason, but now one thing led to another until causality was dead. Quantum mechanics made everything finally random, things can go this way or that way, the mathematics deny certainty, they reveal only probability and chance, and Einstein couldn't believe in a God who threw dice. He should have come to me, I would have told him, 'Listen, Albert, He threw *you* – look around, He never stops.' What is a hamster, by the way? No, tell me in a minute, I want to tell you something first. There is a straight ladder from the atom to the grain of sand, and the only real mystery in physics is the missing rung. Below it, particle physics; above it, classical physics; but in between, metaphysics. All the mystery in life turns out to be this same mystery, the join between things which are distinct and yet continuous, body and mind, free will and fate, living cells and life itself; the moment before the foetus. Who needed God when everything worked like billiard balls? (*He laughs quietly to himself.*) The man who took the certainty out of Newton was Einstein. *Da!* He supplied the dice. If there's no God it's a terrible waste of a good joke. What were you going to say?

HAPGOOD: It's like a fat rabbit with no ears.

KERNER: Oh yes. You mean a *khomyak*.

HAPGOOD: Yes, a *khomyak* called Roger. (*Pause.*) Joseph, after this thing with Ridley you're blown, you know, your career will be over.

KERNER: Except as a scientist, you mean.

HAPGOOD: Yes, that's what I mean, I won't need you any more, I mean I'll need you again – oh, *sugar!* – you *know* what I mean – do you want to marry me? I think I'd like to be married. Well, don't look like that.

KERNER: What is this? – because of a photograph? It is not even necessary, I never look at it.

HAPGOOD: Won't you want to meet him now?

KERNER: Oh, yes. 'This is Joe.' 'Hello, young man.'

HAPGOOD: (*Defiantly*) Well, I'm going to tell him, whether you marry me or not.

KERNER: I'm not charmed by this. If I loved you it was so long ago I had to tell you in Russian and you kept the tape running. It was not a safe house for love. The spy was falling in love with the case-officer, you could hear it on the playback. One day you switched off the hidden microphone and got pregnant.

HAPGOOD: That's uncalled for. I loved you.

KERNER: You interrogated me. Weeks, months, every day. I was your thought, your objective . . . If love was like that it would not even be healthy.

HAPGOOD: (*Stubbornly*) I loved you, Joseph.

KERNER: You fell into your own honeypot –

HAPGOOD: (*Flares*) That's a damned lie! You unspeakable *cad*!

KERNER: – and *now* you think you'd like to be married, and tell Joe he has a father after all, not dead after all, only a secret, we are all in the secret service! – no, I don't think so. And suppose I decided to return.

(*That brings her up short.*)

HAPGOOD: Where? Why would you do that?

KERNER: *Toska po rodine.*

HAPGOOD: You mustn't say that to me, Joseph. Please don't say it.

(KERNER *comforts her.*)

KERNER: Milaya moya, rodnaya moya . . . it's all right. I am your Joe.

(*She suffers his embrace, then softens into it.*)

Cad is good. I like cad.

HAPGOOD: Honeypot . . .

KERNER: Is that wrong?

HAPGOOD: Honey*trap*. And anyway that's something else. You and your books. I don't think I'm going to marry you after all.

KERNER: I thought you would marry Paul.

(*Wrong.* HAPGOOD *stiffens, separates herself.*)

HAPGOOD: I'll see you this evening. And let Paul do the talking. Keep your end of it as simple as you can.

KERNER: Worry about yourself. I will be magnificent.

ACT TWO

SCENE I

Hapgood's office evening.
BLAIR *sits in Hapgood's place.* HAPGOOD *sits to one side.* RIDLEY
sits to the other side. They are waiting. When RIDLEY *gets bored
with this he opens his mouth to say something.*

BLAIR: (*Mildly*) Shut up, Ridley.

> (*The door opens and* MAGGS *comes in with a potted plant, with
> card attached, and delivers it to* HAPGOOD. *She opens the little
> envelope and looks at the florist's card, replaces the card and
> puts the envelope back where it started on the potted plant.
> Meanwhile* MAGGS *receives a nod from* BLAIR *and leaves the
> room, returning immediately to let* KERNER *into the room.*
> MAGGS *retires again closing the door.*)

BLAIR: (*Greeting* KERNER) Joseph!

KERNER: Hello, Paul.

BLAIR: Sit here, won't you?

KERNER: (*Turns to* HAPGOOD.) So. Something special.

> (HAPGOOD *ignores his glance. After a slight pause,* KERNER
> *takes the chair down-table opposite* BLAIR.)

BLAIR: This is a friendly interview. That's a technical term. It
means it is not a hostile interview, which is also a technical
term. I'll define them if you wish. (*Pause.*) Well, I won't
protract this. (*From a dossier he produces about half a dozen
five-by-eight black and white photographs; pages from a
typewritten document.*) Have a look at these, would you?
(*He pushes them down the table to* KERNER *who spreads them
face up in front of him.*)
I'm afraid they're not very good – photographs of
photographs – but you can probably see what they are.

KERNER: Of course.

BLAIR: One of your bi-monthly reports on the anti-matter
programme you're running with the Centre for Nuclear
Research in Geneva, April/May: copies to the main
contractors, the Livermore Research Laboratory in

California, through the SDI office in the Pentagon, travelling by embassy courier from Grosvenor Square; and copies to the Defence Liaison Committee, also by hand; both lots under the control of this office, where indeed the copies are made; a very limited circulation, fifteen copies in all, nine American and six British. In fact, however, these photographs are of a British copy. The white patch is the erasure of the circulation number printed on to each copy *ab origine*. Washington adds an American circulation prefix, missing from these pages but not erased. All clear so far?

KERNER: Where did the photos come from?

BLAIR: Moscow. They were received in Washington three days ago from an American agent in place, not an *American*, of course; 'in place' means –

KERNER: Please, I am not illiterate.

BLAIR: The six British copies have a read-and-return distribution of eleven. That includes the Minister, the Liaison Committee and the Prime Minister's box. It doesn't include your lab, or this office where our copy is kept on file with the turnkeys.

KERNER: May I ask a question?

BLAIR: Yes, do.

KERNER: Why are you sitting in Mrs Hapgood's chair?

BLAIR: That is a very fair question. The answer is that Mrs Hapgood isn't here. Mr Ridley isn't here either. They are on paid leave, which is why they can't be with us this evening, and which is why this is a friendly interview.

KERNER: (*Laughs.*) Oh, Paul, how unlike you – and how happy it makes me. Have you broken the rules at last? – turned by a pair of pretty eyelashes?

HAPGOOD: (*Cross*) I don't have to take that, Joseph.

KERNER: I'm sorry, I meant Ridley.

HAPGOOD: Behave yourself, damn you!

BLAIR: (*Intervenes calmingly*) Please . . . As you know, there is a regular traffic of monitored information going to the Soviets from this office, organized and prepared by Mrs Hapgood and Mr Ridley, and delivered to you for delivery to your

Russian control. In other words a channel already exists. As a precautionary measure, Mrs Hapgood and Mr Ridley have been relieved of their duties. In the same spirit of caution rather than insinuation, your research programme will have to be interrupted for a while, in the national interest. Notice of your own suspension will reach you by messenger at eight o'clock in the morning.

KERNER: Paul, listen – you don't know how many people get their hands on this . . . my lab – the Whitehall secretariat, the turnkeys, the Minister's wife, his mistress – who knows? – also it could be an American Embassy copy before it receives the Washington prefix. There's probably fifty, sixty people. The channel means nothing.

BLAIR: The pages were photographed on some kind of table-top, I expect a little hurriedly as is often the way in these affairs. The last page – photograph number six – is not well framed. You can see how it happens: the pages were pinned together at top left and turned over one by one, and the five turned pages have twisted the sixth page a little askew. The frame has caught the edge of a further document lying underneath. (*He reaches into his dossier again and produces another photograph which he slides down the table.*) This is the enlargement. Essentially it's a photograph of part of the right-hand edge of a set of numerical tables. It is in fact a set of angular distributions of neutron production on a uranium target in a cyclotron, whatever that may be and I don't want you to tell me. The important point is that it derives from the print-out of the raw material received here from you. It is not part of the bi-monthly report which is prepared for ignorant folk like ministers and generals. Taking the two documents together, we are talking about something which has a circulation of three, which is why I thought I'd bring you together for a chat, just between ourselves for the moment. (*He includes* HAPGOOD *and* RIDLEY *who stay expressionless.*) I'm sorry it's awkward for you and Mrs Hapgood but these things have to be faced.

KERNER: (*Indicating* RIDLEY) What about him? Isn't it awkward for him?

BLAIR: Yes, but not in isolation. For reasons I can go into if you wish. Ridley – Mr Ridley – and Mrs Hapgood are tied together on this one, for better or worse. (*Pause.*) Well, I'll explain, then.

KERNER: No, it is not necessary.
(*He pushes the photographs back towards* BLAIR.)
Not hurried, only careless.

HAPGOOD: (*Just conversation*) Joseph, don't do this. I don't need it. Tell the truth.

KERNER: The truth is what Paul knows it is.

HAPGOOD: (*To* BLAIR) He's lying to you because he thinks it's me.
(BLAIR *waits.* HAPGOOD *starts to lose control of her tone.*)
Oh, wake up, Paul! Why would he? (*To* KERNER) Why would you? Why would you give away your work?

KERNER: Because it's mine to give. Whose did you think it was? Yours? Who are you? You and Blair? Dog-catchers. And now you think I am your dog – be careful the dog didn't catch you.

HAPGOOD: Don't give me that! (*To* BLAIR) He's not a triple, you know damn well he's not a triple –

KERNER: (*Laughs, not kindly.*) Pride. And your certainty is also amusing – you think you have seen to the bottom of things, but there is no bottom. I cannot see it, and you think you are cleverer than me? What I see at the moment is greed and chauvinism, the appropriation of knowledge for political domination.

HAPGOOD: (*Losing her temper*) What is this bilge? – are you telling me that's how he talks? We spent months getting inside his head, he's a physics freak and a maverick, the Russians picked him for this because he had a good defector profile and he didn't fool us, he fooled them, he despises the Soviets, he couldn't sell himself that stuff and he has no reason to. *He has no reason* – give me his reason.

KERNER: They found out about Joe.

(*Pause.* HAPGOOD *poleaxed, as it were.* BLAIR *stays level.*)
Sorry.

BLAIR: How?

KERNER: I don't know.

BLAIR: When?

KERNER: More than a year. They came to me and said, 'Well,
so you have a child with your British case-officer. OK –
congratulations, we were stupid, but now it is time to mend
the damage. For the sake of the boy.'

BLAIR: What did they mean by that?

KERNER: What do *you* think, Paul? I didn't ask. (*To* HAPGOOD)
I had to, Lilya.

HAPGOOD: Joseph. All you had to do was tell me.

KERNER: That is naïve. (*To* BLAIR) Not just the bi-monthly
reports. You should know this.

BLAIR: What else?

KERNER: My programme.

BLAIR: This trap business?

KERNER: They had the trap, they had the laser optics for
handling the particles. They couldn't put it together –
nobody could put it together because when you cool it to
near-absolute zero –

BLAIR: Joseph – get to it.

KERNER: Everything was halted, it was like needing two trains
to arrive together on the same line without destroying each
other.

BLAIR: So it couldn't be done?

KERNER: Oh, yes. Like many things which are very difficult it
turned out to be not so difficult if you have the right
thought. These things are not, after all, trains, they are
very small and they travel at nearly the speed of light, so
relativity effects are absolutely real and things that are
simultaneous to one observer are not simultaneous to
another observer. Everybody knew that was the way to do
it but nobody could tidy it up until I was fortunate to have
the right thought, and now it was possible to make an
experiment with my thought. I worked out the programme

for this.

BLAIR: Did they know that?

KERNER: No, we are speaking at last summer. June. I
continued to give them other lines of inquiry, they
continued to ask after the health of the boy. You
understand. But last month was the Geneva test and my
programme was good. It could not be contained, of course;
a good result is the gossip of the scientific world, and it was
the end of the dance for me and my Soviet control. They
said I had lied, broken the bargain, they said it was an
ultimatum now, or they would take my son, and they
absolutely would have taken him.

BLAIR: So you gave it to them.

KERNER: Of course.

HAPGOOD: Paul –

BLAIR: I know. Let me. (*To* KERNER) But the only meet you've
had since your Geneva test was yesterday.

KERNER: I mean yesterday. At the pool.

BLAIR: At the pool? How did you deliver?

KERNER: On disc.

BLAIR: But that was a chickenfeed disc – we cleared the print-
out.

KERNER: No, it was on the boot-tracks.

BLAIR: Explain that.

KERNER: The normal readout was the chickenfeed. There was a
key-code for the hidden files.

(HAPGOOD *stands up*.)

BLAIR: (*To* HAPGOOD) Stay calm. (*He presses the intercom*.)
Maggs – come in.

KERNER: What is the matter?

(MAGGS *enters from his office*.)

BLAIR: (*Calmly*) Oh, Maggs . . . get Mrs Hapgood's son to the
phone, would you? – headmaster, matron, anybody, but
fast.

(HAPGOOD *unfreezes*.)

HAPGOOD: I'll call the payphone, his dorm hasn't gone up.

KERNER: It's all right – they don't want him now –

BLAIR: Go, Maggs!

MAGGS: But Joe isn't there, sir . . . Merryweather came back. Joe wasn't in school – he had permission . . . well, Mrs Hapgood sent for him to be picked up, the driver had a letter –

BLAIR: Merryweather?

MAGGS: He came back at about half past three. (*To* HAPGOOD) I'm sorry . . . I didn't know you'd be out – it's in your box –

HAPGOOD: *Oh, Christ*, Maggs.

BLAIR: (*To* MAGGS) Go and check.

(MAGGS *goes out.* HAPGOOD *has found* MERRYWEATHER's *message in her in-tray. It is in a sealed envelope which she opens.*)

KERNER: But I gave them everything –

BLAIR: I'm afraid not –

KERNER: Yes I did – I delivered –

BLAIR: Stop talking, Joseph – we intercepted your delivery, they never got your disc.

KERNER: You blowed it! You bloody fool!

(RIDLEY *seems to be out of it. He approaches the desk and picks up the photoframe and looks at it for a moment.*)

RIDLEY: (*To himself*) God almighty.

(BLAIR *goes to the door and opens it.*)

BLAIR: (*Shouts*) Maggs!

HAPGOOD: (*Calmly enough*) He isn't there, Paul.

(*She has been looking at the contents of* MERRYWEATHER's *message.*)

KERNER: (*To* HAPGOOD) They won't hurt him, they'll want to trade.

BLAIR: I know that but we can't trade.

(*To* HAPGOOD) He's not harmed, he's in a safe house with babysitters – you *know* that. They'll find a way to talk to you and I'll have every side of this covered, but it won't even come to that – it's a local initiative and a stupid one, it's going to be stopped from the Moscow end, I promise you, the diplomatic route and no nonsense –

KERNER: (*Loud*) Don't do that – they can't admit to a thing
like this.

BLAIR: You're out of it now –

KERNER: You will put them in a corner –

BLAIR: Then they can crawl out of it –

HAPGOOD: For God's sake shut up!

(*It has become a row.*)

RIDLEY: Why don't we just give it to them? What does it
matter? Wait for the call and make the trade. If it comes
tonight make it tonight, a kid like that, he should be in bed
anyway, we can all get some sleep.

Look, what are we talking about? Are we talking about a
list of agents in place? Are we talking about blowing the
work names? the batting order in Half Moon Street? the
cover jobs in the Moscow Embassy? Any of those and all
right, the boy maybe has to take his chances. But what has
Kerner got? (*Derisively*) The solution to the anti-particle
trap! Since when was the anti-particle trap a problem?

BLAIR: Shut up, Ridley. (*To* HAPGOOD) I'll take that disc.

RIDLEY: Don't give it to him.

BLAIR: Ridley, you're out of line.

RIDLEY: (*Loses his temper*) Don't tell me I'm out of line, I know
about this and you don't know fuck, all you know is to talk
Greek. Kerner is supposed to be the one with brains and he
doesn't have enough to know he's pimping fantasies for
people with none. There's nothing on that disc except
physics and it will stay physics till little Hapgood is a
merchant banker. *There is no gadget here. It has no use.* It's
the instructions for one go on a billion pound train set, and
that's all it is. Space defence, my arse. (*To* KERNER)
Listen, you tell them the first time I say something which
isn't true and I'll stop. Livermore thinks it can make an
X-ray laser to knock out a ballistic missile and Kerner's bit
of this is a new kind of percussion cap for the bullet: when
the bullet is a laser you need a percussion cap like an
H-bomb, one bomb per bullet, naturally it destroys the gun
as well as the target but what the hell, all right, you trigger

the bomb and the X-rays will lase for you, and if you can do it by putting matter together with anti-matter you get a nice clean bang, no fallout, and Kerner gets the Peace Prize. Leave aside that all the particle accelerators on earth produce no more anti-matter in a year than will make a bang like twenty pounds of dynamite. Leave aside that to make the system work up there in the sky you need about fifty million lines of information code and at NASA they can't handle half a million without launch delays and the Russians probably wouldn't wait. Leave everything aside and there's still the problem that Kerner's bullet can't shoot inside the earth's atmosphere. The gun in the sky is no good for anything except ICBMs coming up through the ceiling, and you've got five minutes because after that your target has turned into eighteen bombs hidden in a hundred decoys and a million bits of tinfoil – and *that's* only until the Russians work out the fast-burn booster which will give you a fighting window of sixty seconds. I mean, this is the military application of Kerner's physics if you're looking ten years ahead, minimum. It's a joke. I'd trade it for my cat if I had a cat. (*To* BLAIR) And you'll blanket this operation and play ransom games with the little bugger – for what? Do you think you won't screw it up?

BLAIR: (*To* HAPGOOD, *as though it's just the two of them*) There isn't a *choice*. I'm running this and I'm not giving you a choice. You have to trust me.

(*Pause.* HAPGOOD *opens a drawer in her desk, takes out the electronic 'key', opens the safe, removes a disc-box, closes the safe, gives the box to* BLAIR.)

(*Going; to* KERNER) You're with me.

KERNER: Lilya . . .

HAPGOOD: Do everything Paul says.

(KERNER *follows* BLAIR *out, leaving the door open.* HAPGOOD *sits quietly, looking at nothing.* RIDLEY *doesn't quite know what to do with himself.*)

RIDLEY: Sorry.

(*He gets up and moves towards the door.*)

HAPGOOD: Ridley, close the door. (RIDLEY *closes the door*.)
    I gave him the dummy.

RIDLEY: What?

HAPGOOD: I gave him the dummy disc from your briefcase.

RIDLEY: Christ almighty.

HAPGOOD: If you don't like it you'd better say.

RIDLEY: Like it or not we can't do it, we'll never be clear.

HAPGOOD: We're already in front. They made contact – Blair
    missed it.

RIDLEY: How?

HAPGOOD: (*Taking the card from the potted plant*) Interflora.
    'Mum – I'll phone tomorrow, two o'clock.' I thought – it's
    not Mother's Day.

RIDLEY: Listen – tell Blair. It's no good without him – he'll
    have the watchers outside your flat before you get home,
    you'll be babysat like the Queen of England, nothing will
    reach you, there'll be a tap on your phone and on every line
    into this building.

HAPGOOD: Except this one (*the red one*). It's the one Joe will tell
    them, he knows the trip-code. I've always broken the rules.

RIDLEY: And what then? You won't be able to go to the
    bathroom, let alone a meet.

HAPGOOD: I know all of that.

RIDLEY: That's if Blair isn't sitting here when the call comes in,
    he'll go where you go.

HAPGOOD: I won't be here. You'll be here.

RIDLEY: Jesus, *I* can't answer it. It has to be you.

HAPGOOD: It will be me.

RIDLEY: You can't be in two places at once.

HAPGOOD: (*Suddenly out of patience*) I'm not busking, Ridley, I
    know how to do this, so is it you and me or not?
    (*Pause.* RIDLEY *nods*.)
    I'll need two or three hours. Have you got a radio?

RIDLEY: Not with me.
    (HAPGOOD *takes her radio out of her bag and gives it to him*.)

HAPGOOD: I'll reach you on it: don't try to talk to me on
    anything else. Don't go home, go to a hotel.

RIDLEY: Mother, I know what to do. (*He goes to leave.*) Will you be all right?

HAPGOOD: (*Nods.*) Stay close.

RIDLEY: It's all right, I'm with you.

(*But she spoils it for him.*)

HAPGOOD: That thing's got a two-mile range, stay close.

(RIDLEY *nods and goes, closing the door.*

HAPGOOD *waits. She opens a desk drawer and takes out another radio. She lays the radio on the desk and waits again. The radio must have a blink-light; perhaps we can see it.*

HAPGOOD *picks it up.*)

HAPGOOD: (*To* RADIO) Is he clear?

RADIO: Green.

(*To* RADIO) I'm here to be told.

(*She puts the radio back on the desk. She starts dialling on the red telephone.*

MAGGS *enters, wearing a topcoat.*)

MAGGS: Good night, Mrs Hapgood.

HAPGOOD: Good night, Maggs. Thank you.

MAGGS: I won't ask.

HAPGOOD: That's right, Maggs. By the way, I won't be in tomorrow.

MAGGS: I'll hold the fort.

(MAGGS *leaves closing the door.*)

HAPGOOD: (*Into phone, brightly*) Hello! Who's that? . . . Sandilands! Can you tell Hapgood it's his mother? Wait a minute, aren't you the one who sells boots? . . . Only the once, I see . . . no, no, it's all right – perfectly all right, in fact quite reasonable, I thought, you can't get much for a pound nowadays . . . *Two pounds?* . . . But surely . . . ? Oh, a pound *each* – well, fair enough, yes, I can see that . . . Yes, darling, I'll hold on for him –

(*In the middle of all that* BLAIR *has quietly entered the room and is collecting the contents of his dossier, sorting things out, putting them away.*)

(*Mutters, derisive*) Merchant banker . . .

BLAIR: You know, you're going to get into such trouble one day

... *I mean, that's the Downing Street one-to-one red line* –
what are they supposed to think when they pick it up and
it's *engaged*?

HAPGOOD: Oh God, so it is. (*Huffily*) It's a perfectly natural
mistake, Joe uses it far more than they do.

BLAIR: That's my point.

HAPGOOD: (*With spirit*) Well I can't give him my work number,
it's an official secret –

BLAIR: (*Grumbling*) You use the security link with Ottawa to
play chess, you arrive in Vienna after dog-legging through
Amsterdam on a false passport and then proceed to send
postcards home as if you're on bloody holiday, you use an
intelligence officer on government time to dispatch football
boots around the Home Counties . . . For someone who's
so safe you're incredibly, I don't know, there's a little
anarchist inside you, I wish you wouldn't . . .

HAPGOOD: Don't be cross, I'm tired.
(*Into phone*) Oh – thank you, Sandilands – I'll hang on –
Paul . . .

BLAIR: Mm?

HAPGOOD: I know this isn't necessary and don't start getting
cross again, I –

BLAIR: (*Somehow irritated, apparently*) It's all right, it's done –

HAPGOOD: You don't know what I –

BLAIR: Yes, yes, watchers at the school till this thing is over,
and Cotton has joined the ground-staff, marking out the
rugger pitches, do him good, he was looking a bit pasty.

HAPGOOD: I absolutely refuse to live without you, do you
understand that?

BLAIR: Of course.
You know, it's going to be tricky doing the swap without a
boy to swap.

HAPGOOD: Well, we'll just have to do the best we can, won't
we?

BLAIR: Of course.

HAPGOOD: (*Into phone*) Oh, hello, Joe! Are you all right,
darling?

(KERNER *enters*.)

KERNER: Magnificent.

BLAIR: Thank you.

KERNER: No, me. You were terrible. I never believed a word of it.

HAPGOOD: (*Into the phone*) No, it was just to tell you not to phone tomorrow in case you were going to. I'm away.

BLAIR: (*To* KERNER) Not even the photographs?

HAPGOOD: (*Into phone*) Oh, good.

KERNER: The photographs I liked.

BLAIR: Yes?

HAPGOOD: (*Into phone*) In the hutch? Well, I was nearly right.
  (*Meanwhile* KERNER *has poured three tots of vodka into the cups.*)
  Thank you, Joseph.
  (KERNER *and* BLAIR *toast each other and knock back the vodka.*)
  (*Into phone*) Well, you're daft – do they fit? . . .

BLAIR: (*To* KERNER) Come on, then.
  (BLAIR *puts his cup down and leaves the room.* KERNER *closes the door after him and remains in the room.*)

HAPGOOD: (*Into phone*) That's all right . . . when is Saturday?
  The day after tomorrow . . . well, probably, I might.
  Home or away?
  (KERNER *gently takes the phone from her and listens to the phone for a few moments and then gives it back to her, and leaves the room.*)
  (*Into phone*) Yes, I'm here. Yes, all right. Well, let me know on Saturday morning.
  Yes, Joe, I'm here to be told.
  (*She puts the phone down.*)

SCENE 2

Now we are in a new place. The first and obvious thing about it is that it is a photographer's studio. The second thing is that it is also where somebody lives; the room is skimpily furnished as a living

*room. There is a front door and also another closable door leading to
the other rooms in what is evidently the photographer's flat. There is
a telephone.*

It is mid-morning. The room is empty. The doorbell rings.

HAPGOOD *comes flying out from the other door. We haven't seen her
like this. She is as different from her other self as the flat is different
from her office; the office being rather cleaner, tidier, and better
organized.* HAPGOOD *opens the front door, and it's* RIDLEY.
RIDLEY *has been shopping: glossy Bond Street carrier bags. He
stares at her.*

RIDLEY: Mrs Newton?

HAPGOOD: (*Casually*) Oh, shit.

RIDLEY: I'm Ernest.

HAPGOOD: Well, you're not what I want, so keep your clothes
    on. Stupid bugger! Not you, darling, come in anyway. (*She
    is already heading for the telephone.*) What did they do? Pick
    you from the catalogue? I'll try and sort it out – charge
    them for half a day if it looks like their fault – it won't be
    the first time – (*Now into the phone*) It's Celia, I want Fred.
    Would you mind not wandering around.

    (*Her last remark needs explaining.* RIDLEY *has dropped his
    parcels and is now, frankly, casing the joint. He is not taking a
    lot of notice of her. He moves around coolly as if he owns the
    place, and in due course he leaves the room, disappearing
    through the 'kitchen door'.*)

    (*Into the phone*) Hello, darling, you're losing your grip – I
    said a Roman soldier, not an Italian waiter, and also he
    looks queer to me . . . Don't tell me what I mean, you're
    gay, he's queer, he's got a queer look about him. He won't
    sell bamboo shoots to a fucking panda, never mind boxer
    shorts . . . Well, I'll look at his body and let you know –
    Fred? – Have you gone? – No, the phone clicked – (*She
    looks around and finds that the room is empty.*)
    Hey – ? What's his name? (*She calls out*) Victor!
    (RIDLEY *wanders back into the room.*)

RIDLEY: (*Casual*) Hang up.

HAPGOOD: What do you think you're doing? (*Into phone*) Is he a
regular? . . . Well, I don't fancy him –
(*That's as far as the phone call gets because* RIDLEY, *still
maintaining a sort of thoughtful cruise, disconnects the call.*)
Now, listen –
(*He looks at her. She goes from fear to relief.*)
You're Betty's friend. Bloody hell, you gave me a turn. I
thought, this isn't Victor, this is a nutter, it's the
Kensington strangler, God, I am sorry, darling, I'm Celia,
don't be offended, being rude about the models is the
house style, it saves a lot of nonsense about being paid for
the reshoot if it needs one, and anyway you do look like an
Italian waiter. What does Betty want? – I don't owe her
any favours, she never does me any, I mean there must be
lots of photographic work going in the spy racket. She says
I won't keep my mouth shut – I'm going to blab that I'm
working for MI5 to everybody I meet? – Is it five or six? –
Can you smell burning? – Oh, sod!
(*She leaves the room in a hurry.* RIDLEY *has been looking at
her like somebody looking at a picture in a gallery. He reaches
into his jacket and produces his radio.*)

RIDLEY: (*To* RADIO) Mother.

HAPGOOD: (*On* RADIO) Ridley.

RIDLEY: You're out of your fucking mind.

HAPGOOD: (*On* RADIO) What's the matter?

RIDLEY: She may be your twin but there the resemblance ends.
She's a pot-head, it reeks, she's growing the stuff in the
window-box, she won't stop talking, she bites her nails, she
looks like shit, I mean it doesn't *begin* . . .

HAPGOOD: (*On* RADIO) Ridley –

RIDLEY: Yeh, all right . . .

HAPGOOD: (*On* RADIO) Where is she?

RIDLEY: In the kitchen burning things . . .

HAPGOOD: (*On* RADIO) I'm signing off.

RIDLEY: No, listen –
(*But evidently she has cut him off. He puts his radio away and
goes to pick up his shopping. He puts it on the sofa, perhaps,*)

and anyway, starts unloading the carrier bags. They are full of clothes in tissue paper. There's also a shoe box and other stuff. It all adds up to one outfit, suitable for the office.
While he is doing this HAPGOOD *bangs her way back into the room (she probably wouldn't have bothered to close the door so a door on a spring might be useful).*
She is nibbling the unburned portion of a croissant, which rapidly gets as far as the wastepaper basket.)

HAPGOOD: And you made me warm my croissant to a frazzle. What have you got there?

RIDLEY: Clothes, shoes, make-up . . . Is there a bathroom?

HAPGOOD: No, we pee in the sink. Can you try to show a little charm?

RIDLEY: Your sister said do what he tells you.

HAPGOOD: So what?

RIDLEY: Run a bath.

HAPGOOD: Why?

RIDLEY: You look as if you need one.

HAPGOOD: Now just a minute –

RIDLEY: And wash your hair.

HAPGOOD: *Just a minute*. I'm not going to a party, I've got a busy morning.

RIDLEY: Victor isn't coming. It's ten twenty and we're leaving here at one fifteen, just under three hours. I'll explain as you go.

HAPGOOD: Will you indeed. (*She picks up the phone again and starts dialling.*)

RIDLEY: Who are you calling?

HAPGOOD: I want to talk to Betty.

(*Without hurrying much, because she is still dialling,* RIDLEY *yanks the phone cord which comes away from the wall bringing fragments of plastic and bits of skirting-board with it.*)

RIDLEY: You don't talk to Betty, you don't talk to anybody, in fact you don't talk so much in general, and you don't swear at all, get used to it, please.

HAPGOOD: You bloody gangster, that telephone is my livelihood!

RIDLEY: Is that right? You'll have to fall back on photography.

HAPGOOD: You're pushing your luck.

RIDLEY: We'll see.

(*He takes a wad of bank notes out of one pocket.*)

That's one thousand pounds.

(*He takes a similar wad out of another pocket.*)

So's this. That's now, this is later.

HAPGOOD: What is it for?

RIDLEY: It's for looking nice and not talking dirty, and answering a telephone. After that, we'll see.

HAPGOOD: Why?

RIDLEY: I'll tell you when it's time.

HAPGOOD: Then why would I do it?

RIDLEY: For the money, your sister said. I want to know about you and your sister, sibling bribery is a new one on me.

HAPGOOD: Well, you can stick this up your –

RIDLEY: Every time you swear I'm taking £10 out of this bundle. You'll get what's left.

HAPGOOD: (*Compromising*) Bum?

(RIDLEY *separates a £10 note from the bundle of money [which is perhaps secured by a rubberband], and puts the remainder back into his pocket.*)

That's theft.

RIDLEY: No, it's arson. (*Because his hand has come out of his pocket with his cigarette lighter with which he sets fire to the note.*)

HAPGOOD: My God, you *are* a nutter. You're all nutters. I knew it then. Is Betty in trouble?

RIDLEY: When?

HAPGOOD: If she's in trouble, I don't mind helping.

RIDLEY: You knew it when?

HAPGOOD: Whenever – fifteen, all those years ago when we did the interviews.

RIDLEY: Tell me about that.

HAPGOOD: I failed the attitude test. Betty was exactly their cup of tea so they kept her anyway.

RIDLEY: Anyway?

HAPGOOD: They were seeing twins – it was a phase. Nutters is not the word. Ask Betty, they had a reason, she'll know what it was. Well, that cheered you up. (*It has.*)

RIDLEY: Yes. Will you have a bath and talk nice and do what I tell you?

HAPGOOD: Is it her money?

RIDLEY: Not exactly.

HAPGOOD: I wouldn't take it if it was hers.

RIDLEY: Fine. It's ten twenty-five.

HAPGOOD: What did you say your name was?

RIDLEY: Ernest. Do you want me to scrub your back?

HAPGOOD: No, thank you. I think I liked you better when you were edgy.

RIDLEY: Take the clothes. They're for you to put on.
(*She gathers them up to take them out.*)

HAPGOOD: They're not really me.

RIDLEY: That's right.
(HAPGOOD *leaves the room.* RIDLEY *stays where he is. The next time he moves, he's somebody else.*)

INTER-SCENE

So we lose the last set without losing RIDLEY. *When the set has gone,* RIDLEY *is in some other place . . . which may be a railway station, or alternatively a place where boats come in, or an airport; whatever the design will take, really. The main thing is that he is a man arriving somewhere. He carries a suitcase. He is a different* RIDLEY.
It's like a quantum jump.
And now we lose him. Perhaps he walks out. Perhaps the scene change has been continuous and he is now erased by its completion.

SCENE 3

BLAIR *and* KERNER *are at the zoo.*

BLAIR: I must confess I always thought that one Ridley was

enough and occasionally surplus to an ideal arrangement of the universe. Now we've got one in Kensington and one who could be anywhere. I imagine he doesn't hang around, he'd come in and out as required. Could be on a British passport, more likely not. This is, of course, assuming that he exists. At the moment it's only an idea.

KERNER: It is not an *idea*, it is not like 'do as you would be done by', or 'steam engine'!, nobody has to have it, the problem has it. The solution is the problem interrogated.

BLAIR: Does it prove twins?

KERNER: No. An invisible man is also a correct solution.

BLAIR: You chaps.

KERNER: Mathematics does not make pictures of the world it only reveals itself. What you make of it – twins, waves, the dark star – is your bet on reality. In Athens, in Paris and at the swimming pool, two Ridleys satisfies a requirement. He was his own alibi. So we're betting on twins. But we need to be lucky also. We need the black panther to cross our path.

BLAIR: You chaps don't believe in that.

KERNER: Oh, we chaps! Niels Bohr lived in a house with a horseshoe on the wall. When people cried, for God's sake, Niels, surely *you* don't believe a horseshoe brings you luck!, he said, no, of course not, but I'm told it works even if you don't believe it.

(BLAIR *continues to look grave.*)

What is the matter, Paul?

BLAIR: Those photographs. Think of Ridley sitting there. He's been sending film to Moscow and now here are these prints, spread out on the table, courtesy of the Washington pouch. Awkward moment for him. And yet, suddenly he's in the clear. Kerner owns up. Well, we can't have Ridley sitting there wondering why you're owning up to his pictures. Ridley knew this wasn't his batch, because he photographed his pages flat, separately; they weren't pinned together by the corners and turned over. And those figures peeping out underneath, the whatsit production in the cyclone-whatever, they were nothing to do with him.

KERNER: I assumed naturally they were not the Moscow pictures.

BLAIR: Did you? And yet the figures ought to have looked like Moscow figures, Joseph. They had been pulled together from different sets, the way somebody might collate the material at the receiving end. (*Pause.*) It really upsets me, Joseph, that you never said, 'Paul, where did you get that photo? Those cycleclip numbers look as if they were assembled at the Moscow end and I'm surprised they had the figures to do it.' I mean, that is assuming you would be surprised.

KERNER: Cyclotron, Paul. It's a sensible word. Cycleclip is bizarre by comparison. (*Pause.*) So now I am a prime suspect – I love that phrase, it's in nearly all the books. A prime is a number which cannot be divided except by itself, and all the suspects are prime; threes and fives, sevens, elevens . . . But really suspects are like squares, the product of twin roots, fours, nines, sixteens . . . what is the square root of sixteen?

BLAIR: Is this a trick question?

KERNER: For you, probably.

BLAIR: Four, then.

KERNER: Correct. But also minus four. Two correct answers. Positive and negative. I am very fond of that minus, it is why I am what I am, I mean not as a suspect but as a physicist. Literally. I am an alchemist of energy and mass, I can turn one into the other and back again, because energy is mass multiplied by the speed of light squared. But the famous equation was not precisely found in its famous form, it was really the *square* of that, and E equals MC squared is the square root. But, of course, so is E equals *minus* MC squared, an equally correct solution . . . just like with your sixteen. Nobody took any notice of the minus for years, it didn't seem to mean anything, there was nothing to which it belonged, you'd need a minus-world, an anti-world, with all the charges reversed, positive for negative, negative for positive. But finally someone trusted the mathematics and said – Well, maybe there is anti-matter as well as matter; anti-atoms made of anti-particles. And lo!, they started to find them. And so on, et cetera, until . . . here I am, Joseph Kerner, the anti-matter man at the zoo. (*Pause.*) I'm not going to help you, you know. Yes – no, either – or . . . You have been too long in the spy business, you think everybody has no secret or one big secret, they are what they seem or they are the opposite. You look at me and think: *Which is he?* Plus or minus? If only you could figure it out like looking into me to find my root. And then you still wouldn't know. We're all doubles. Even you. Your cover is Bachelor of Arts first class, with an amusing incomprehension of the sciences, but you insist on laboratory standards for reality, while I insist on its artfulness. So it is with us all, we're not so one-or-the-other. The one who puts on the clothes in the morning is the working majority, but at night – perhaps in the moment before unconsciousness – we meet our sleeper – the priest is visited by the doubter, the Marxist sees the civilizing force of the bourgeoisie, the captain of industry admits the justice of common ownership.

BLAIR: And you – what do you admit?

KERNER: My estrangement.

BLAIR: I'm sorry.

KERNER: I'm thinking of going home, you know.

BLAIR: No, I didn't know. It may be tricky for you.

KERNER: Do you mean leaving or arriving?

BLAIR: That's roughly what I'm asking *you*.

KERNER: Of course. Either-or. Dog or dog-catcher. I don't even know if I was a genuine defector. When they recruited me, it is true that I had already thought of getting out, but to be honest the system I wanted to flee was the vacuum tube logic system. We were using computers which you had in museums. I wasn't seeking asylum, I was seeking an IBM one-nine-five.

BLAIR: No, you were ours, Joseph. They put you up to it, but

Elizabeth turned you. You were her joe.

KERNER: Yes, I was. There is something appalling about love. It uses up all one's moral judgement. Afterwards it is like returning to a system of values, or at least to the attempt.

BLAIR: (*Angrily*) Yes, values. It's not all bloody computers, is it?

KERNER: No. The West is morally superior, in my opinion. It is in different degrees unjust and corrupt like the East. Its moral superiority lies in the fact that the system contains the possibility of its own reversal – I am enthralled by the voting, to me it has power of an equation in nature, the masses converted to energy. Highly theoretical, of course, but it means the responsibility is everybody's, you cannot pass the blame to a few gangsters. I prefer that but I don't need to live with my preference. My friend Georgi has offered to arrange things if I want to go.

BLAIR: Why are you telling me?

KERNER: I declined his offer.

BLAIR: I'm glad, Joseph.

KERNER: I prefer British Airways.

(*Pause.*)

BLAIR: You should have accepted.

KERNER: (*Angrily*) Oh, yes! – You don't want to look, and then you'll get spy pattern!

BLAIR: I like to know what's what.

KERNER: Of course! Objective reality.

BLAIR: (*Angrily*) What other kind is there? You're this or you're that, and you know which. Physics is a detail I can't afford, I've got one of my people working the inside lane on false papers and if she's been set up I'll feed you to the crocodiles – is that *real* enough for you?

KERNER: One of your *people*? Oh, Paul. *You* would betray her before I would. My mamushka.

BLAIR: Good. Good, Joseph.

(*He seems pleased by the way that went.*)

Now. Is the sister thing going to work?

KERNER: Oh, yes. I was afraid of it, but with Mr Ridley it will be all right.

(*He starts to leave, pauses.*)

I never saw Elizabeth sleeping. Interrogation hours, you know. She said, 'I want to *sleep* with you'. But she never did. And when I learned to read English books I realized that she never said it, either.

(KERNER *walks away.*)

SCENE 4

Hapgood's office. It's empty.

The door is opened with a key from the outside. RIDLEY *enters the office.*

RIDLEY: (*Addressing* HAPGOOD *outside*) Move.

HAPGOOD *enters behind him. She is wearing the clothes which he brought to the flat.*

RIDLEY *closes the door.* HAPGOOD *looks around.*

RIDLEY *has a bag, perhaps a sports holdall.*

RIDLEY: Sit there. (RIDLEY *does everything smoothly and quickly. He riffles through a stack of printed documents [technical magazines perhaps] on the desk and extracts a sealed envelope, which he tears open. It contains a small key and a scribble.*)

HAPGOOD: What if somebody comes in?

RIDLEY: It's your office, for God's sake.

(*He gives her the key.*)

Middle drawer.

(HAPGOOD *uses the key to open the middle drawer of the desk.*)

Remote key.

HAPGOOD: This?

(*She shows him the electronic key for the safe.* RIDLEY *takes it. He consults the scribble, programmes the key, opens the safe. From the safe he takes a disc-box – a new one, i.e. a sealed once-only box of the same type. He closes the safe. He puts the disc-box into his bag, together with the torn envelope and the scribble. During this:*)

Are you going to tell me what I'm doing here?

74

RIDLEY: Sure. Any phone that rings, don't pick it up. I'll pick
  it up.

  (*He picks up the red telephone, looks at its underneath, puts it
  down again; from the bag he takes a simple 'eavesdrop'
  connection, a single ear-piece ready to be wired up into a
  telephone receiver; and a screwdriver.*

  At that moment, the door opens and MAGGS *walks in, with a
  file, much as yesterday.*)

MAGGS: Good afternoon Mrs Hapgood, you came in after all.
  Do you want to see the decrypts?

  (HAPGOOD *looks at* RIDLEY.)

RIDLEY: Hello, Maggs . . . aren't you supposed to be having
  lunch?

MAGGS: Yes, sir.

RIDLEY: Well, piss off then. Go to the pub.

MAGGS: I was in the pub. (*To* HAPGOOD) I got the desk to
  bleep me if you came in – just the top one, really, it's
  green-routed and Sydney's been on twice this morning.

HAPGOOD: Has he?

MAGGS: Sydney – they only want a yes or no.

RIDLEY: Let them wait.

HAPGOOD: No, I can do that.

RIDLEY: Are you sure, Mother?

HAPGOOD: What's the matter with you today, Ridley?

  (HAPGOOD *takes the 'top one' from* MAGGS *and peruses it with
  interest.*)

  Mm . . .

RIDLEY: Perhaps you'd like me to . . .

  (*He reaches for it.* MAGGS *glances at him.*)

MAGGS: It's yo-yo, Mrs Hapgood.

HAPGOOD: Is it, is it really? Yes, indeed. It's yo-yo, Ridley, you
  know what yo-yo is.

RIDLEY: Yes.

HAPGOOD: What?

RIDLEY: (*Grimly*) 'Your eyes only'.

HAPGOOD: There you are, then. Fascinating.

MAGGS: Just a yes or no.

75

HAPGOOD: Yes! Definitely yes!

(*She passes the paper smartly back to* MAGGS.)

Thank you, Maggs. I'll do the rest later.

MAGGS: McPherson came in if you want it.

HAPGOOD: Really?

RIDLEY: It's five minutes to two, Mother.

HAPGOOD: I want to know about McPherson.

MAGGS: Bishop to queen two.

(*Pause.*)

HAPGOOD: Right.

RIDLEY: *Mother.*

HAPGOOD: Yes. Now you can piss off.

(*The world ends for* MAGGS, *just for a moment. The red phone rings.* MAGGS *lifts it up.*)

MAGGS: (*To phone*) Mrs Hapgood's office . . . just a moment.

(*He gives the phone to* HAPGOOD *and leaves.*)

RIDLEY: Shit!

HAPGOOD: What do I do?

RIDLEY: Talk!

(RIDLEY *has two desperate concerns: to wire up his 'eavesdrop' and to prompt* HAPGOOD. *But it's hopeless, a mess.*)

HAPGOOD: (*To phone*) Hello . . . yes, it's her, it's me . . .

RIDLEY: '*I want to talk to Joe!*' . . . '*I want to talk to Joe!*'

HAPGOOD: (*Covering the phone*) I can't hear! (*Into phone*) Yes . . . Eleven thirty . . . (*To* RIDLEY) Someone wants a meeting.

RIDLEY: Where? Keep them talking, ask for Joe . . .

HAPGOOD: Yes . . . Where? . . . Right . . .

(RIDLEY *is nowhere near ready when she puts the phone down.*)

RIDLEY: I'll kill you for this! – Eleven thirty where? *Where?*

(HAPGOOD *is still contemplating the phone warily.*)

HAPGOOD: Ten Downing Street.

RIDLEY: *What?* Oh, Jesus!

HAPGOOD: Was that it?

RIDLEY: No. I thought they were early.

HAPGOOD: Who's Joe?

(RIDLEY *ignores her, he works on the red phone.*)

Listen, I can't do this if you don't tell me what I'm doing.

RIDLEY: I'll tell you when it's time to tell you. God almighty
. . . I ought to slap you bow-legged.

HAPGOOD: You don't mean Betty's Joe, do you? Ernie?

RIDLEY: Ridley.

HAPGOOD: Ridley. What's the silly cow been up to?

RIDLEY: Don't you like her?

HAPGOOD: Of course I like her, she's my sister.

(RIDLEY *completes his work, and pauses to consider her. He's
unsettled, somehow thrown by seeing her in this office, in these
clothes . . . She is so obviously* HAPGOOD.)

RIDLEY: Mrs Newton. What happened to *him*? You're
divorced?

HAPGOOD: I'll say. Bastard owes me thousands. Actually it was
Mr Newton who did for Betty and me. She said he'd go
bad, warned me off, sister to sister. So I crossed her off my
list and married him. Then he went bad. So of course I
never forgave her.

Do you mean she plays chess without a board?

RIDLEY: Looks like it.

HAPGOOD: That sounds like her.

RIDLEY: She's something.

HAPGOOD: Showing off, I meant.

RIDLEY: Why aren't you close?

HAPGOOD: Well, she was always the scholarship girl and I was
the delinquent. Having the kid was good for her, she
always thought the delinquents had the bastards and the
scholarship girls had the wedding. It shook up her view of
the world, slightly.

RIDLEY: Do you know the father?

HAPGOOD: Do *you* know? Well, I don't see why I should tell
you, if *she* hasn't.

RIDLEY: Have you met him?

HAPGOOD: No.

RIDLEY: You don't know.

HAPGOOD: Do you mind if I light up?

RIDLEY: She doesn't smoke.

HAPGOOD: It's all right, it's not a real cigarette.

(*She puts a home-made cigarette in her mouth;* RIDLEY *snatches it away and keeps it.*)

RIDLEY: For God's sake, don't you know where you are?

HAPGOOD: So what do we do now?

RIDLEY: (*Looking at his watch*) We wait. (*He leans over to reach the buttons on Hapgood's desk.*)

When I do this (*he snaps his fingers*), you say, 'No calls, Maggs, no interruptions.'

(*He snaps his fingers.*)

HAPGOOD: No calls, Maggs, no interruptions.

MAGGS'S VOICE: Yes, ma'am.

(*Satisfied for the moment, but nervy,* RIDLEY *paces.*)

HAPGOOD: He probably thinks . . .

RIDLEY: Yeh, nice thought.

HAPGOOD: Speak for yourself.

RIDLEY: I was.

HAPGOOD: Don't fancy your fuckin' chances.

(*Pacing,* RIDLEY, *as though absentmindedly, takes the bundle of money out of his pocket, detaches a £10 note and sets fire to it with his lighter. He carries on pacing, she carries on looking at him.*)

Sit down, for God's sake.

(RIDLEY *sits at the table.*)

Ten of hearts.

RIDLEY: What about it?

HAPGOOD: Ten of hearts – now you.

(RIDLEY *sighs.*)

RIDLEY: King of hearts.

HAPGOOD: Two of clubs.

RIDLEY: Well, what are we playing?

HAPGOOD: Go on.

RIDLEY: Ace of spades.

HAPGOOD: Seven of diamonds.

RIDLEY: Haven't you got any spades?

HAPGOOD: Play your cards.

RIDLEY: Six of hearts.

HAPGOOD: Two of hearts.

RIDLEY: This is stupid. Nine of clubs.

HAPGOOD: Jack of clubs.

RIDLEY: Jack of spades.

HAPGOOD: *Snap!!* Bad luck . . .

(RIDLEY *jumps irritatedly to his feet, and then the red phone rings*.)

RIDLEY: *Leave it!*

Listen – Betty's Joe has been kidnapped – this is the people who took him.

(*He takes her left hand, calmly, lays it palm-down on the desk, and using his own hand as a blade he chops her hand across the knuckles, with coolly judged force, enough to make her cry out with pain.*)

RIDLEY: You want to talk to Joe – where's Joe, where's Joe?

(*He lifts the red phone now and puts it into her right hand, meanwhile putting the extra earpiece to his ear.* HAPGOOD *is whimpering and disoriented.*)

HAPGOOD: (*Into phone*) Hello, where's Joe, I want to talk to Joe – I – Yes – yes – yes –

Yes. I heard – can I talk to –

(RIDLEY *relaxes. He takes the phone from her gently and replaces it. The phone call has taken perhaps fifteen seconds.*

HAPGOOD *springs away from the desk, from him, crying, comforting her injured hand.*)

RIDLEY: You were very good!

HAPGOOD: You bloody maniac!

(RIDLEY *is disconnecting his eavesdrop, replacing everything into his bag.*)

Where's Betty? – is it true about Joe?

RIDLEY: Yes, it's true. But we'll get him back. Eight hours to kill.

(RIDLEY *retrieves her cigarette from his pocket, lights it and puts it in her mouth.*

HAPGOOD *draws on the cigarette, still shocked, trembling, settling down.*)

You were fine. I'm sorry I hurt you. We can go now. Me first. Count twelve and I'll see you outside.

(RIDLEY *picks up his bag. Carefully he takes away her cigarette, takes a drag himself, and keeps the cigarette. He opens the door.*)

Welcome to the firm.

(RIDLEY *leaves.*

Left alone, HAPGOOD *relaxes, although her hand is still painful.* MAGGS *enters anxious.*)

MAGGS: Is everything all right, Mrs Hapgood?

HAPGOOD: Yes, Maggs – everything's fine.

(*She heads through the open door.*)

Queen to king one.

MAGGS: (*Following her out.*) Queen to king one.

SCENE 5

A cheap hotel room. It is evening; dark. Perhaps a neon sign outside.

HAPGOOD, *fully dressed, has gone to sleep on the bed.* RIDLEY *stands watching her. Perhaps he is changing into the clothes which he will wear in the next scene.*

RIDLEY *takes out his radio.*

RIDLEY: (*To* RADIO) Mother.

(*No answer.*)

(*To* RADIO) Mother.

(*No answer.*)

(*Louder to* RADIO) Mother – where the hell are you!

(HAPGOOD, *on the bed, has stirred awake.*)

HAPGOOD: How much longer?

RIDLEY: A couple of hours.

(*He put his radio away and takes his gun out of his holster and checks it.*)

HAPGOOD: Ernest . . . I hardly dare ask you this, but is your mother in the secret service too?

(RIDLEY *ignores that. He puts his gun back into the holster.*)

What's that for, Ernie?

RIDLEY: It's for killing people. It's a gun.

HAPGOOD: Do you kill people, Ernie?

RIDLEY: You'll be the second.

HAPGOOD: Well, I don't want to do this. Why don't we just tell the police?

RIDLEY: Christ, you're stupid.

HAPGOOD: The police must know where the Russians live, they can't live anywhere they like can they?

RIDLEY: What bloody Russians? I think it's me who's stupid. Somebody's lying to somebody. They're lying to her or she's lying to me.

HAPGOOD: I don't think Betty tells lies.

RIDLEY: Telling lies is Betty's job, sweetheart – lies, fraud, entrapment, blackmail, sometimes people die, or get stuck in *gulags* till their parents are dead and their kids have kids, so Betty can know something which the opposition thinks she doesn't know, most of which doesn't matter a fuck, and that's just the half they didn't *plant* on her – so she's lucky if she comes out better than even, that's the edge she's in it for, and if she's thinking now it wasn't worth one sleepless night for her little prep-school boy, good for her, she had it coming.

HAPGOOD: Maybe she did.

RIDLEY: She should have given him a daddy instead of getting her buzz out of running joes to please an old bastard who doesn't want her and never will – (*a thought strikes him, strikes him as funny*) Blair's been running *her* for years!

HAPGOOD: What do you mean, Ernest?

RIDLEY: She got pregnant screwing the Russians, Auntie. Then it was a choice between losing a daddy and losing a prize double, a turned mole who would have been blown overnight if he was known to be the father, and we aren't in the daddy business, we're in the mole business.

HAPGOOD: I don't know what you're talking about – *talk English*!

RIDLEY: Your sister carries a torch and she can't tell front from arseholes. We're in a racket which identifies the national interest with the interests of the officer class. Betty bought the whole lie and put it first, she *is* the lie. I'll get her kid back for her but it's only personal. If she's set me up I'll kill her.

HAPGOOD: You're potty about her, Ernest. I'm disappointed in you. Why should she set you up? What for? Somebody isn't lying to somebody, everybody's lying to everybody. You're all at it. Liars. Nutters' corner. You deserve each other – *she* shouldn't be out without a guide dog, and *you* don't know if you're carrying a torch for her or a gun. Secret bloody service! If you're *it* I'm learning Russian. And you sound as if you're half-way through the course, no wonder you're confused. You're out on a limb for a boy she put there, while she was making the world safe for him to talk properly in and play the game – what a pal, I should have a friend like you.

RIDLEY: It's not her fault. Do you think you cracked it taking snaps of fancy junk? She's all right. Anyway, I like kids, and you never know, now and again someone is telling the truth.

HAPGOOD: You're all right, Ernest. You're just not her type.

RIDLEY: Yeh, she says I'm not safe. Too damned right I'm not. If I was safe I wouldn't be in a whore's hotel with somebody's auntie waiting for a meet that smells like a dead mackerel.

HAPGOOD: Where would you be?

RIDLEY: Anywhere I like, with a solid gold box for a ticket.

HAPGOOD: You can walk away, Ernie, it's only skirt.

RIDLEY: Shut up.

HAPGOOD: (*Cranking up*) You'd better be sure, she plays without a board. You haven't got a prayer.

RIDLEY: *Shut up!*

HAPGOOD: If you think she's lying, walk away. If you think bringing back her son will make you her *type*, walk away. You won't get in the money, women like her don't pay out – take my advice and open the box.

RIDLEY: (*Grabbing her*) *Who the hell are you?*

HAPGOOD: I'm your dreamgirl, Ernie – Hapgood without the
brains or the taste.

>   (*She is without resistance, and he takes, without the niceties;
>   his kiss looks as if it might draw blood.*)

SCENE 6

*The pool. Night. Empty. A towel hangs over the door of Cubicle
One (any cubicle).*

It is dark. RIDLEY (TWO) *enters from the lobby carrying a large
torch. He looks around with the help of the torch. He moves upstage.
We see only the torch now. The torch-beam comes back towards us.*
RIDLEY (ONE) *walks into the beam. He has come from the showers
(depending on the layout). He carries the sports bag. He approaches
the torch. The two men embrace briefly. Our* RIDLEY *remains: the
one with the torch retires. (The torch, of course, changed hands
upstage – here and subsequently we only clearly see, and only hear,
the actor who plays* RIDLEY.)

RIDLEY *now opens his holdall, takes out a disc-box and posts it
under the door with the towel on it. He removes the towel and enters
Cubicle Two. He hangs the towel over that door.*

HAPGOOD *enters from the lobby. She pauses, timid.*

HAPGOOD: Ernest . . . ?

>   (RIDLEY *with the torch, reveals himself.*)

RIDLEY: It's OK. Call the boy.

>   (HAPGOOD *hesitates.*)

>   Call the boy.

HAPGOOD: Joe . . .

JOE: (*Out of sight*) Mummy . . . ?

>   (*He appears from upstage in the cubicle area.* HAPGOOD *moves
>   to where she can see him.*)

HAPGOOD: Hello, darling. It's all right.

RIDLEY: Stay there, Joe.

>   (JOE *halts.*)

>   Do it.

(HAPGOOD *opens her bag, takes the disc-box from it, and posts it under the door of Cubicle Two [where the towel hangs]. She pulls the towel down and tosses it over the door into the cubicle. She comes back to* JOE *and takes his hand.*)

HAPGOOD: Off we go.

(HAPGOOD *takes* JOE *out through the lobby doors, followed by* RIDLEY.

When they have gone RIDLEY (TWO) *comes out of Cubicle Two, holding the towel and the disc which* HAPGOOD *had posted. He takes the towel to Cubicle One, where it had originally hung, and tosses it over the door. The door of the cubicle opens.* WATES *is inside.* WATES *has a gun.*)

WATES: (*Just conversation*) Hey, Ridley. Here's what you do. You walk, you don't talk.

(WATES *walks* RIDLEY *upstage into the dark cubicle area. Pause.* BLAIR *comes from upstage and approaches Cubicle One. He takes from the cubicle the disc which had been posted there.* BLAIR *moves out towards the lobby but before he gets there* RIDLEY *comes in.* RIDLEY *is amused.*)

BLAIR: (*Greeting*) Ridley.

(RIDLEY *laughs.*)

RIDLEY: It never smelled Russian, not for a minute. It smelled of private profit. No wonder the kidnap was so clean. Uncle Paul. What a breeze.

BLAIR: Except . . . surely . . .

RIDLEY: Except the boy will tell. I'm thinking.

BLAIR: I should.

RIDLEY: There was no kidnap.

BLAIR: Better.

RIDLEY: There was never any kidnap. You and Hapgood.

BLAIR: Much better.

RIDLEY: You and Hapgood. Make it look right, make a mug of me and the sister, and afterwards both of you back in place like china dogs on the mantelpiece.

BLAIR: Now you've lost me. Something about a sister.

RIDLEY: The sister is perfect, I know about this. She's here and she's not here.

BLAIR: I keep thinking you said sister.

(HAPGOOD *has now come in quietly from the lobby*.)

Surely you know Mrs Hapgood?

RIDLEY: I know her sister better. (*To* HAPGOOD) Don't I?

(*She gives nothing away*.)

Give me a minute, I'm slow.

(*A* RADIO *talks, softly, briefly. It is in* HAPGOOD'S *hand. She raises it to her mouth*.)

HAPGOOD: Mother.

RADIO: Are we green?

HAPGOOD: Green.

RADIO: You know it's twins?

HAPGOOD: Yes, I know it's twins.

(*She puts the radio in her bag*.)

RIDLEY: Listen, be yourself. These people are not for you, in the end they get it all wrong, the dustbins are gaping for them. Him most. He's had enough out of you and you're getting nothing back, he's dry and you're the juice. We can walk out of here, Auntie.

HAPGOOD: You should have opened the box.

RIDLEY: I could have walked away with it any time and let the boy take his chances. This way you got both, my treat.

HAPGOOD: There was nothing in there except a bleep.

(*Pause*.)

RIDLEY: Well, now I don't know which one you are. One of them can shoot and one of them can –

HAPGOOD: Don't Ridley –

(RIDLEY *is going to kill her, as promised. Everything goes into slow motion, beginning with and including the sound of* HAPGOOD'S *gun, lasting probably five seconds.* RIDLEY *has got as far as taking his gun out when* HAPGOOD *shoots him. Meanwhile,* WATES *is leaning into view, upstage, slightly late, gun in hand. Strobe lighting.*

BLAIR *doesn't move.*

Meanwhile the cubicles are disappearing, and we are to find ourselves outside rather than inside the lobby doors. If the doors themselves remain, the sign 'Men' is no longer reversed.

85

RIDLEY (*i.e. his body*) *is erased along with the cubicles and becomes a body on a stretcher, the face covered by a blanket. The gunshot and the strobe extend through this scene change. At the end of the change we are left with* HAPGOOD, BLAIR *and* WATES, *the stretcher with stretcher bearers, and the* RIDLEY TWIN, *handcuffed, under arrest, being led away.* RIDLEY, *passing the stretcher, manages to look at the face under the blanket. He cries out indistinctly and is led away (by* MERRYWEATHER).

There is the flashing blue light of an ambulance off-stage. All this happens swiftly, continuously from the gunshot.)

BLAIR: (*To* WATES *angrily*) Where were *you*?

WATES: I was second, he was third.

(*To* HAPGOOD) Oh, you *mother*.

BLAIR: (*To* WATES) I want that ambulance out of here.

WATES: No rush.

HAPGOOD: Ben – ? It was the shoulder.

WATES: No, ma'am.

HAPGOOD: It was the shoulder.

WATES: I'm sorry. You were a little low. It's not like targets.
(*Pause.* HAPGOOD *moves a few paces towards where the stretcher left and then comes back to* WATES.)

HAPGOOD: Ben, thank you for your co-operation.
(*They shake hands.*)

WATES: You bet.
(WATES *leaves.*)

BLAIR: Come on Elizabeth, Joe's waiting.

HAPGOOD: (*Tense with anger*) Don't even talk to me. We said we'd do it without Joe.

BLAIR: It had to look right.

HAPGOOD: You lied to me.

BLAIR: Without the boy it wouldn't have looked right.

HAPGOOD: I was willing to risk it.

BLAIR: I wasn't.

HAPGOOD: I'll never forgive you for that, never ever.

BLAIR: I know that. I knew that.
(*Pause. Her anger starts dispersing into misery.*)

HAPGOOD: And what am I supposed to tell him?

BLAIR: Tell him it's a secret. The secret service. Small boys
understand that.

HAPGOOD: What do you know about small boys?

BLAIR: Well, I was one.

HAPGOOD: I'll come in when he's asleep. We'll save what we
can. Perhaps you can tee up some communication.

BLAIR: I've done that.

HAPGOOD: Paul –

BLAIR: No, no, you'll get over it.

HAPGOOD: No.

BLAIR: What about your network?

HAPGOOD: *What network?!* Ridley's blown it inside out! I'm
pulling people out like chestnuts and I don't know the
stooges from the doubles. Christ, Paul, I must have been
buying nothing but lies and chickenfeed since Joe was in
his pram! I'm not blaming you about Joe. The truth is I
enjoyed it and now I've stopped.

BLAIR: (*With asperity*) Why am I supposed to feel sorry for Joe?
There's worse things. I'd feel a damn sight sorrier for
anyone who didn't know there was an either-or and we
can't afford to lose. One has to pick oneself up and carry
on. It's them or us, isn't it?

HAPGOOD: Who? Us and the KGB? The opposition! We're just
keeping each other in business, we should send each other
Christmas cards – oh, f-f-fuck it, Paul!
(*So that's that.*

BLAIR *turns away, hesitates and leaves. The next time*
HAPGOOD *moves she is standing by the rugby pitch.*)

SCENE 7

HAPGOOD *stands on the touchline. She isn't looking at much.*
KERNER *is standing some way behind her, wearing an overcoat.*
Some rugby sounds.
KERNER *comes down to join her.*

HAPGOOD *sees him.*

HAPGOOD: Joseph . . . You came to say hello?
KERNER: On the contrary. (*He looks front, a bit puzzled.
    Gamely*) Interesting.
HAPGOOD: It hasn't started yet. They're just practising.
KERNER: Oh yes, which one is he?
HAPGOOD: (*Pointing*) New rugby boots. I'm awfully glad to see
    you.
KERNER: (*Spotting him*) Oh, yes.
HAPGOOD: He'll come over when they take their tracksuits off.
    I tried to find you this morning.
KERNER: I was buying my ticket. Also a suitcase.
HAPGOOD: I heard you've been sending your luggage on ahead
    for months. Does Paul know why?
KERNER: (*Shrugs*) Paul thinks I was a triple, but I was definitely
    not, I was past that, quadruple at least, maybe quintuple.
HAPGOOD: They found out about Joe, didn't they? They turned
    you back again. You made up the truth.
KERNER: It's nothing to worry, you know.
HAPGOOD: I'm not worried. I'm out of it now. This is him.
    (JOE *runs in, wearing his tracksuit, which he takes off now.
    His rugger kit is clean. The new boots.*)
JOE: Hello, Mum.
HAPGOOD: Good luck, darling. This is Mr Kerner – Joseph.
    Another Joe.
JOE: Hello, sir.
KERNER: Hello. How are you?
JOE: All rights'a, thankyous'a. (*To* HAPGOOD) Will you be here
    after?
HAPGOOD: Yes, see you later.
    (*She has the tracksuit. Perhaps the top half goes round her
    neck.* JOE *runs off. Pause.*) That was him.
KERNER: Very nice. Very English. (*Pause.*) Of course, he *is* half
    English, one forgets that. Well . . . good.
HAPGOOD: Do you want to stay for tea? They lay it on for
    parents.

KERNER: Better not, I think.

HAPGOOD: Oh, Joe.

(*She breaks down. He holds her, awkwardly.*)

HAPGOOD: Prosty, Josef.*

KERNER: Da nyet – vyet u menya byl vybar, Lilichka.

HAPGOOD: Nyet tagda u tibya nye bylo vybora –

KERNER: Da – mu ya pashol . . . ya napishu kagda dayedu . . .

(KERNER *kisses her and starts to leave.*)

HAPGOOD: How can you go? *How can you?*

(*She turns away. The game starts. Referee's whistle, the kick. After a few moments* HAPGOOD *collects herself and takes notice of the rugby.*

When the game starts KERNER's *interest is snagged. He stops and looks at the game.*)

HAPGOOD: Come on St Christopher's! – We can win this one! Get those tackles in!

(*She turns round and finds that* KERNER *is still there. She turns back to the game and comes alive.*)

HAPGOOD: Shove! – heel! – well heeled! – well out! – move it! – *move it, Hapgood!* – that's good – that's *better*!

---

*HAPGOOD: I'm sorry, Joseph.
KERNER: No, no. I had a choice too, Lilychka.
HAPGOOD: You had no choice then.
KERNER: Yes, I'd better go. I'll write when I get there.